You Can ...

EXPECT A

MIRACLE

13 Keys To Becoming A

Miracle Magnet

DR JOHN HINWOOD

with

Dr Judy Hinwood

EAM

EAM Publishing

You Can ... Expect A Miracle
13 Keys To Becoming A Miracle Magnet

Dr John Hinwood
Website: www.expectamiracle.com

Published by
EAM Publishing
PO Box 4125
Forest Lake, Qld, 4078
Australia
Phone: +61 7 3879 0069
Email: admin@expectamiracle.com

ISBN: 978-0-9872805-2-7

Cover design by: idrewdesign

Why not use Drs John & Judy Hinwood as guest speakers for your next conference or seminar?

EXPECT A MIRACLE SCHOOL Pty Ltd

PO Box 4125, Forest Lake 4078, Queensland, AUSTRALIA

Tel: +61 7 3879 0069
Fax: +61 7 3714 9700
Email: info@expectamiracle.com
Website: www.expectamiracle.com

Drs John & Judy Hinwood have an unusual way of changing people's lives. In a journey over the past 26 Years they have been handing out a small white card to people they have met. The card has just three words written on it ...

"Expect A Miracle". They have handed out over 95,000 cards to people all over the world in the last 26 years. Through this small act of giving the Hinwood's prompt people to think about their own miracles; the small, seemingly insignificant events and moments in people's lives that open the doors to a sense of wonderment and opportunity.

John & Judy Hinwood are sought-after international conference speakers and they run public events all over the world.

As international speakers they inspire their audiences into taking practical action steps to move their lives to new levels. Their perspectives, humour, observations, insights into life and entertaining stories are from the heart and they inspire and motivate people into taking positive action steps.

The inspirational You Can EXPECT A MIRACLE book series are giving many people around the world hope and a good dose of positivity.

Also by Drs John & Judy Hinwood

Expect A Miracle Cards
Expect A Miracle card packs

Live Events
Creating Miracles In Your Life (1 hour)
The Miracle Mindset (2 hours)
Expect A Miracle School (Half Day)
Stress To Strength (2 Day Workshop)

Webinars ... Streamed
Creating Miracles in Your Life
The Miracle Mindset
Expect A Miracle School

Books
You Can EXPECT A MIRACLE ... The Book To Change Your Life
You Can EXPECT A MIRACLE ... Yes YOU Can
You Can EXPECT A MIRACLE ... Unexpected Miracles
You Can EXPECT A MIRACLE ... With Chiropractic
You Can EXPECT A MIRACLE ... Insights Into Life
You Can EXPECT A MIRACLE ... 201 Miracle Messages from A to Z
You Can EXPECT A MIRACLE ... 13 Keys to Becoming A Miracle Magnet
STRESS TO STRENGTH ... Mind Tools To Calm, Connect and Create

Audio Programs ... CD & Streamed
Creating Miracles in Your Life
The Miracle Mindset
Expect A Miracle School

Online Programs
Stress to Strength Alliance ... Via email and webinar
Stress to Strength ... Powerful Steps – 23 days
Stress to Strength ... Final Keys – 49 days
Stress to Strength Coaching Program

Practitioner Training

Stress to Strength Practitioner ... 12 month Cert IV program

www.expectamiracle.com

You Can Expect A Miracle
13 Keys To Becoming A Miracle Magnet

Table of Contents

If you have the courage to persist in going for what you really want in life, you will often get it.

Find time to just sit and put your brain into freewheeling mode. Just let it run free ... busy brains sometimes miss miracles!

Help enough others get their miracles and it's amazing what a positive life you create.

Abundance abounds ... there are plenty of miracles for us all.

When you are totally open to receiving miracles, it's astounding how they find their way to you and you become a 'miracle magnet'.

Miracles come when you least expect them ... make them welcome whenever they arrive.

Start telling people you come into contact with to Expect A Miracle. This will work like a boomerang and come back to you as you continue to spread the miracle expectancy.

This book is dedicated to the late Dr John Thie who taught me an extremely valuable lesson in life...

"A job worth doing is worth doing lousy!"

If we just make a start and get into motion, then the miracles can happen.

Acknowledgements

The idea for this book came to me during the afternoon breakout session of the third *Expect A Miracle* School I held in my home town of Brisbane, Australia in February 2012. A participant asked me when I was doing a book signing of my popular first book; YOU CAN *EXPECT A MIRACLE... The Book to Change Your Life,* "is what you're doing today going to be another future book?" My answer was, "what a great idea!"

Thank you to the kind soul who felt compelled to ask me that special question.

Thank you to my beautiful wife and best mate of forty five years Judy who has been my back of room and seminar logistics director for *Expect A Miracle School.* She knows the thirteen keys to becoming a miracle magnet very well as we have honed them time and time again in many of our brainstorming sessions.

As Judy understands these keys so well and lives her life based on them, I asked would she like to be the support author on this project. My rock solid mate and amazing support person said, "Absolutely!" She continually encouraged me to write about my thoughts and experiences in creating a clear and grounding guidebook of miracle creation keys.

Thank you to my Personal Assistant Di Girot who typed, edited, retyped and made suggestions during the preparation of each of the thirteen keys.

Thank you to my friend John Milne who commented on the content and provided editing support and guidance.

Thank you Drew whose creative genius is responsible for the covers of all six books we are currently releasing. He has a flair for creating an image for the cover that reflects the essence of the stories in the book.

I am grateful to my friend Dr Danny Drubin, author of the best seller *Letting Go of Your Bananas,* for his generosity in providing the endorsement quote on the front cover of the book. Danny is one of those individuals who naturally is a 'miracle magnet'.

www.expectamiracle.com

Foreword

You Can EXPECT A MIRACLE... 13 Keys To Becoming A Miracle Magnet is an exciting concept that once understood by the student, will see expecting the best as the outcome when positive expectations, natural talent and constructive action meet.

Expectation is a state of mind and heart. Great things can happen when people are open to possibilities and alternatives. There is room for ideas big and small.

Expectation is an act of will. Expecting is more than a passive state or a stationary bus picking up passengers. It involves strength of will. Its brother is intent. Its sister is purpose.

Expectation means commitment. Expecting the best becomes a way of life. Have you ever met a person who lives in joyful expectation? You see it in their shining eyes.

Expectation looks forward. It looks for new horizons. It seeks the path of improvement or growth. It makes a better family, community or workplace.

Expectation comes with her partner Serendipity. People call them chance meetings, unexpected contacts, seed thoughts even miracles. Recognize them when you meet them.

Expectation provides a connection. Sharing expectations can open doors of insight, build bridges of collaboration, heal old hurts. The power lies in the giving and the receiving.

Expectation speaks the language of encouragement. Using words that build people up creates a positive picture of a shared future.

Wildly unrealistic expectations will defy logic. They will disappoint and disillusion you. Avoid the snake oil sales person who builds unrealistic expectations of quick profits, a certain promotion or an easy life without work or pain. Life is not like that. Our expectations need to be in harmony with who we are; the talents we possess; the vocation we are called to. Hold on to expectations that have a "ring of truth".

Expectation joins the energy flow of the universe. As a writer, I start each day slowly unfolding ideas like a surprise present. I find myself floating in the swiftly flowing river of creativity. The skills I have mastered build confidence and buoy my spirits.

By expecting the best you will welcome the good things in life. By reaching out to like-minded people you will be blessed beyond measure. By giving more than you get, you will always have enough. In days of trouble and pain you will find new hope.

Expect the best and you'll be surprised how often you will experience it.

Dr John Hinwood has lived a life full of miracles for over sixty years and the 13 Keys he teaches in this book have been tried, tested and proven successfully for years by him personally and so many others around the world.

John Milne
Author, Speaker, Executive Coach
Brisbane, Australia

Introduction

The reason that I use the late Dr John Thei's statement... "A job worth doing is worth doing lousy!" is to awaken people who are sitting on the side lines in life waiting for miracles to happen. In the main they are stuck in many areas of their life because they had the statement drummed into them as a young child... "A job worth doing is worth doing well!"

Miracles will not happen in people's lives on a regular basis until they participate in the game of life at all levels. Getting started at something new is often a problem and painful for most people and brings up all types of fear. Do you ever hear yourself using these fearful expressions? I won't look good, people will judge me, I'm not prepared enough yet, I don't have enough money, I don't have enough experience. The list is endless.

When I heard John Thei for the first time say... "A job worth doing is worth doing lousy!" in Dallas, Texas in September of 1977 my internal dialogue and mind chatter went into massive judgement. It took me two weeks to work my way through what his message really was. This message so pressed ALL MY BUTTONS!!

It actually challenged my value system in a huge way.

Another quote I use towards the end of Expect A Miracle School is that of Soichiro Honda... "Success is 99% failure." This is what "A job worth doing, is worth doing lousy!" is all about.

If this negative statement is what it takes to shift one person in a seminar room to create miracles in their life then I have achieved my goal.

I interviewed a highly successful American man in his mid-seventies recently when I was speaking in Phuket Thailand and he shared with me that all of the miracles that had happened in his life were really the direct result of his failures. He commented to me how he loved the way I used, "A job worth doing, is worth doing lousy!' to assist people to give themselves permission to make mistakes so they can grow and create miracles in their lives.

Win Borden said..."If you wait to do everything until you're sure it's right, you'll probably never do much of anything."

My message in this book to you through its many stories, is to encourage you to go to the edge, and in the best Australian vernacular, 'have a go', even if you believe you're not quite ready yet.

We all deserve miracles and they are waiting for us to claim them by being an active participant in life, instead of a timid feeder or a 'gunna'!

Enjoy living a life full of miracles. The power is within you!

Miracle 🔑 One

Ask yourself whenever you face a challenge, "What would be the best outcome in this situation?"

GOAL

TAKE
the
ACTION STEPS

GRATITUDE
Say
THANK YOU

CELEBRATE
the
"MIRACLE"

The people who get on in this world are the people who get up and look for the circumstances they want, and, if they can't find them, make them.

George Bernard Shaw

Number One

Miracle step number one is to ask yourself whenever you face a challenge, "what would be the best outcome in this situation?"

So many people actually do achieve their goals, however the problem is that they set the bar so low that they never stretch and push themselves to realize their true dreams in life. Donald Trump said, "It takes as much energy to think small as it does to think big, so why not think big?"

I'm going to share a story with you to explain the power of thinking big, and how you can manifest a goal and create a miracle when you are starting from scratch. The story will demonstrate that you can create what you want in life when it appears on the surface to most people that what you are seeking is not possible to achieve.

In 1978, my wife Judy and I returned to Australia after living overseas for ten years. We'd travelled extensively off the beaten track to many wonderful and remote places around the world for our first five years away. The second five years we spent in Canada, studying chiropractic. I also set up a private practice in Toronto during my last year.

We came back home and had family spread half way around the country in Sydney, Melbourne and Adelaide. We decided to hit the road and drive the south eastern seaboard from Adelaide in South Australia, through Victoria and New South Wales where our family members resided. Our plan was to drive into Queensland if needed and not to go any further north than the Tropic of Capricorn where the sub-tropical climate ends. We had decided that living in the tropics permanently would be too hot and humid for us.

We purchased a station wagon, packed our camping gear and headed out from Sydney driving west over the Great Dividing Range. We left the coast behind us and headed out across the vast western plains of New South Wales into the semi desert of north eastern South Australia and onto its capital, Adelaide.

After some family time in Australia's premier wine country of the day, we commenced our search for the ideal community in which to live and set up practice. On day one of our search, we found a wonderful place at Christies Beach on the edge of Adelaide, and took an option on a possible practice location. We decided that we needed to complete our search route before we made our final decision.

We soaked up daily doses of magnificent coastal and rural landscapes as we weaved our way in and out following the south eastern seaboard of our beautiful continent. This countryside led us to the conclusion that the cities didn't really attract us. We had decided as we journeyed northward, a community of about ten thousand people was what we were seeking.

When we drove into the popular seaside town of Forster on Wallis Lake on the mid north coast of New South Wales three hundred kilometres north of Sydney we both had a gut feeling that this was 'the place'! Seven thousand people; magnificent beaches; the home to eighty percent of Australia's export oysters at that time (I adore oysters); great fishing; known for its lobsters; a beautiful relaxing place and a magnificent thick bush backdrop.

Across the bridge at the entrance to the lake was the sister town of Tuncurry, another little gem of a seaside sleepy village.

When we had set out on our journey from Adelaide weeks before we had decided that we would let our 'gut feeling' be our guide when we arrived in the our dream town. If we both had 'butterflies' and an internal 'knowing' that this was the place where would settle, we would not do a head job on ourselves and allow our educated mind to overrule it.

After driving through three states and some two thousand six hundred kilometres, Forster gave us both those special gut feelings immediately we arrived there.

Here we were, super excited to get going now and we couldn't find any commercial space to rent in town. We visited all the agents, spoke to the Council and asked everyone we spoke to around town. There was nothing coming vacant in the short to medium term either.

What was our possible alternative? We needed a miracle right now.

A savvy real estate agent we met, Don Robson, suggested that as we were a professional healthcare business, we would qualify with Council to run a home-office practice. Out of nowhere, a paradigm shift by this agent, gave us another huge opportunity to explore and find a suitable location to start our business and make a home. I call this a 'miracle thought' as no one at Council informed us of this option or any of the other real estate agents we visited.

A moment later our Agent Don smiled broadly and said, "I have just the place for you. It's going to take some major renovation, but the location is perfect for business and you'll have all the traffic that goes in and out of town pass your door". He went on to tell us that the property was opposite a beautiful small secluded beach just south of the headland where the main beach ended. It had been vacant for quite some time as it was a deceased estate .The family had only decided a few days earlier to auction the property as soon as possible or sell it prior to auction.

Don smiled again and said, "It even gets better for what you want! Actually it is not only one house, it is two houses joined by a covered in walkway with bathrooms, plus five garages out back that could be demolished to easily create a nine car parking lot. It also has a lane way access for the car park and practice entrance. The rear property would be your practice next to the car park. The auction reserve price is forty thousand dollars."

The agent said, "We haven't even listed it yet but if you offer the reserve price you could buy the property today, as its location is within the zone for home office healthcare practices."

Now we had to find the ten thousand dollar deposit; this is where the next miracle was needed.

We went to the bank next door with a big introduction from Don the real estate agent. He explained that we were new chiropractors who had just moved to town after having studied at the world famous Canadian Memorial Chiropractic College in Toronto and we were highly qualified to care for the people of the district. We nodded and sat down with the Bank Manager Mr Don Crighton.

In those days there were very few Canadian trained chiropractors in Australia, and those who were practicing, all had very high reputations as successful chiropractors who were helping many people. Mr Crighton told us of his bad back and bad knee and that he had been told by some customers that he needed to find a Canadian trained chiropractor who would be able to help him.

I did a brief consultation on the spot and a mini physical examination in his office and determined that yes, he was a prospective chiropractic patient and we would be able to care for him as soon as we set up our practice. His prospective healing miracle had arrived in his office that day.

He was so excited and committed to us that he would support us to do whatever was needed finance wise, so we could open our doors as soon as possible.

Applying for a bank loan today is of course the domain of computer networks running banks with lending approvals being made in many cases thousands of kilometres away by the stroke of a key on a computer, by a person totally remote from the borrower. The assessor is relying on a pre set algorithm to make the decision.

Back in 1978 the decision in larger bank branches for loan approvals under say $200,000 was the domain of the bank manager. He could approve them himself provided all standard procedures were followed.

After the pleasantries and giving him our Canadian banking history over the past five years, I said to the Manager, "We don't have any money for a deposit to buy a property". However, we spent the profit I made from my one year in practice in Canada on a new x-ray machine, four top of the range chiropractic adjusting tables, three Dermathermograph infra-red diagnostic scanners and other physical diagnosis equipment and an extensive medical library. Plus we have the cash for a fit out of rented office space.

Mr Crighton asked, "Did I hear you say that you have a new x-ray machine?" I answered, "Yes we do and we also have full darkroom facilities to facilitate immediate processing of the films". He answered, "Our local thirty six bed Hospital doesn't have an x-ray facility. We really need you in town."

Mr Crighton was a lovely fellow and he said, "If you can get ten thousand dollars for the deposit, the bank will lend you the other thirty thousand dollars". He went on to say, "You need to borrow the ten thousand dollars from your parents".

Neither of our parents had the money to lend to us, even if they had been able to, we would not have asked them. The next morning we checked the ads in the financial pages of the *Sydney Morning Herald's* business section. An ad jumped out of the page to greet us... 'Short term loans unsecured to ten thousand dollars'. We drove five hours to Sydney to meet with the financier.

Our meeting with the financier was brief. We showed him our business plan and he said, "Yes, I can lend you ten thousand dollars for ninety days at 40 percent per annum interest rate or ten percent for the ninety day term". We shook hands, signed a letter of agreement, and he gave us $10,000 cash and we drove back to Forster in an extremely excited state. Another miracle achieved on route to our goal.

The next morning we went back to the bank and sat down with the Manager Mr Crighton and presented him with the ten thousand dollars cash deposit on the property. He was excited that we had rounded up the deposit. His immediate statement was, "You must have been borrowed this from your parents, did you?" We didn't answer; we kept on reading the newspaper. He asked the question again. We didn't answer. His next statement was, "Oh yes, I understand, we can now take care of signing the mortgage documents". And so it was, we had just bought our first property in Australia on one hundred percent borrowed funds. In 1978, this was unheard of. Our second miracle was accomplished in establishing our practice.

Mr Crighton then asked us how long it would be before the practice would be open as he really needed our help with his bad back and knee problems. He explained he had been waiting for a good chiropractor to come to town as many people had told him that chiropractors could help. Some people had even told him that a good chiropractor can produce miracles and that was what he was seeking.

It took five weeks for the property to settle and another five weeks for us working long hours with tradesmen to convert the second house into an attractive and very functional office that created great flow. The other house we renovated at the same time as our residence.

We started calling people we had on our waiting list the week before we opened. We made Mr Crighton's appointment mid-morning on the second day before we were booked out. We had patients everywhere and our nine car parking lot was full and he had to park on the street. When I finally sat him down in my office to do his initial consultation he said he was amazed at how professional our office was and he had never expected anything as up-market as we had created. We had the only x-ray facility in town. Amazingly not even the hospital had one.

After his extensive examination, Infra-red scan and x-rays and the hope that he could finally get some relief for his chronic problems, I asked him could we come to the bank during our lunch break as we needed to discuss our rapidly growing business.

When we arrived at the bank, Don Crighton was all smiles and just as excited as we were that the people of Forster and district were so keen to avail themselves of our services. I explained that our projections in the business plan we had given him on our first meeting a couple of months earlier had been rapidly overtaken. What we were doing now on day two of practice, and with our forward bookings of new patients and the care plans that would be generated for each new patient, we were already at the twelve month mark of the business plan.

We explained that we would like a ten thousand dollar business loan so we could make provision for our rapid growth. He explained that as we had only been in business for two days that we didn't qualify for such a loan according to bank rules and policies. However, there was nothing stopping him from giving each of us a five thousand dollar personal loan. And so it was that the bank funded our real estate purchase one hundred percent! This was a miracle unheard of in 1978.

We only worked mornings on Thursday, so at noon we jumped into the car and drove the five hours to Sydney to repay the ten thousand dollar loan to the private financier. At forty percent interest per annum we had to come up with one thousand dollars from our takings for the first three and a half days. It was a breeze!

We learned from this experience that if you step up to the edge when you know what it is that you truly want in life, and you have massive passion to match your desire, then miracles appear to support you.

We didn't say no we can't do it. We didn't say it wasn't possible. We didn't listen to the doomsday people who said that our plan was not possible. We listened to our gut that said with some ingenuity, there is a way here to achieve your goal. Act as if you already own the property. We did that, and it was amazing what happened.

Within three months we opened a branch practice two days a week in a town one hundred and ten kilometres away after requests from the towns-folk. This second practice in picturesque Gloucester also thrived from day one. Judy ran our Forster practice on the two half days that I practiced in Gloucester the two full days. There's nothing like giving a working woman two half days to attend to her home chores.

Two years on it was time to move to a city as we had started post graduate lecturing on weekends for the Preston Institute of Technology chiropractic program. We needed to drive five hours each way to and from Sydney to fly all over Australia to lecture. Our remote location was a beautiful part of the world to live in; however it was starting to prove to be a burden on our professional lecturing life.

As soon as we decided to move, the perfect buyer showed up and we also did very well financially. During our two years in Forster there was a property boom and rampant inflation. We enjoyed one of those dream runs where you buy property low and sell high as well as selling a very successful start up business that was rock solid after two years.

There was an interesting peripheral happening that occurred in chiropractic in Forster that created a miracle for someone else.

The day we first arrived in town we found that there was another chiropractor running a very low key practice. We visited him and when we told him we had already purchased an x-ray machine he told us that it wouldn't work as not even the local hospital had an x-ray facility. He said, "People will just not pay for x-rays here".

Twelve months on after we established our practice, the other chiropractor in town installed his own x-ray machine also. Still the hospital did not have an x-ray facility.

I read a story while studying in Canada that if one lawyer sets up practice in a small rural town there was a good chance they could go bankrupt. If two different lawyers set up two separate practices in the same town, they both usually thrive. There's room for everybody.

Miracles happen in the strangest of ways.

Miracle 🔑 Two

Think, talk and act positively in all circumstances. No matter what !

GOAL

GRATITUDE
Say
THANK YOU

TAKE
the
ACTION STEPS

CELEBRATE
the
"MIRACLE"

When I thought I couldn't go on, I forced myself to keep going.
My success is based on persistence, not luck.

Estee Lauder

Number Two

Think, talk and act positively in all circumstances. No matter what!

This is the key that is centred on the four words, 'I can, I will'.

I will share a story with you about these words and why this miracle key is so important no matter what our age. This lesson first came to me, or I first understood it, at the age of three.

In 1949, my parents took me to the renowned orthopaedic surgeon of the day on Macquarie Street in Sydney, Dr Hugh Barry. This man was a leader in orthopaedic surgery in Australia and the British Commonwealth. Why I was taken to see him?

I was a very active roly-poly three year-old. I was always playing, jumping, and running but all of a sudden, whenever I started to run, really run, I would trip and fall on my face time after time. I had gravel rashes on my knees and face constantly. My parents became very concerned because the preschool head teacher thought I had a problem with my legs.

This was 1949 and polio was epidemic in Australia. Any time a child had limb challenges or pain, people panicked. I was taken to our family doctor, Dr Miller and he said, "Johnny has really bad knock-knees and needs a very good orthopaedist" – at least it wasn't polio.

The specialist was in downtown Sydney in one of those buildings that had a small entrance, were full of medical specialists' rooms, down narrow dark corridors. I was taken into the great man's rooms, stripped down and examined. He had me do all sorts of tests.

At that time my father was the Sporting Editor at the Sydney Daily Mirror newspaper. Sport was my father's life. My mother loved to play tennis and loved sport as well. Dr Barry sat down, looking stern, white coat and all and with all his authority said "Mr and Mrs Hinwood, you need to understand, your boy will never play sport, it's just not possible. Running will never be possible for him. There could be some other things wrong with him as well. I do know that he will never play sport."

My father just put his head down in his hands, rubbed his face and his eyes, and when he took his hands away, I could see tears welling at the corners of his eyes. He was a very stoic man who didn't show his emotion very much normally and he was very, very upset. I had never seen my father in a state like this before. My mother was crying. My father said, "Look doctor, there must be something that can be done, there has to be something that you can do. Just give us something. We'll do anything to help Johnny, anything."

Dr Barry replied," I can give you something but I don't think it will work. You can give it a go if you like, however it has to be done every day and it will take a lot of discipline on your part. You will have to have special aluminium splints made, two for each leg, front and back, from ankle to groin. At night, bath the child and then put his legs into the splints front and back and wrap them in place with crepe bandages. In the morning, take them off. You will need to do this daily for twelve months to have any effect at all."

Continuing he explained. "He will also need prescription orthopaedic boots that he must wear absolutely all the time for two years, no matter what. They are big and awkward but building them up on the inside might train his knees to go outwards again." My parents said, "We'll do it, absolutely."

I remember that moment vividly. There was Dr Hugh Barry sitting, giving his pronouncement to a three year old, that my life was finished as I and my parents saw it; no sport, no running, and I would have a life of restriction and lack, of wishing and watching and sadness for us all. I could never do what other little boys just do. Fancy not being able to play sport when I would be a big boy like Daddy.

Here I was, sitting on my father's knee, seeing and feeling his desperate state. "Only one son and there's a lot of sport for him to enjoy" he said. I looked from this person, to that person. Over there was the extremely negative talk, over here were my parents doing what they could, and here was my positive self-talk. My self-talk said, "That's rubbish... rubbish. I can do this. I'm going to run. I'm going to be an Australian champion at sport by the time I'm a big boy."

My parents participated wonderfully by having the built up boots and splints made and they never missed a night putting on the splints for a year. They made sure that the moment the splints came off each morning that the boots went on. I was never allowed to be barefooted.

 What happened? I started to run at the end of this time. At age fifteen I did become the Australian Junior Judo champion, and at age seventeen I took up a scholarship at Sydney Teachers' College as a physical education teacher. I still run swim and ride, and play sport. I love having an active and healthy body.

It's amazing that if you have the will and just go for it, what can happen. There has to be positive self-talk; think, talk, and act positively no matter what. Was I a clumsy and self-conscious little fellow walking in those boots for two years and uncomfortable in the splints? Was it difficult for my parents to keep me literally toeing the line? It certainly was!

What would my life have been if we hadn't all persevered? It's hard to imagine.

Throughout my life there has been numerous times, which I call 'defining moments'. At these times I have had to step up and act positively. I believe we all have these challenges and opportunities. How grateful I am for my parents' teaching me about positive commitment at such a young age. For the rest of my life I will thank my parents for being people who would not take no for an answer. I told them that many times.

Please continue with handing out Expect A Miracle cards. Write down three more miracles you have seen every day in your diary or in your journal. Go over your goals and action steps to get yourself clear on where you are heading. By doing these things you are going to create your miracle mind set.

Celebrate, "woohooo" when goals large and small are achieved. Give thanks always. Send a written thank you. It is a beautiful way to continue the gratitude process as you move ahead creating your ideal life.

Miracle 🗝 Three

Miracles don't necessarily come with a clap of thunder or a flash of lightning ... sometimes they come on tippy-toe.

GOAL

GRATITUDE
Say
THANK YOU

TAKE
the
ACTION STEPS

CELEBRATE
the
"MIRACLE"

Somewhere in there, among the worries, questions, advice and advertising jingles, lives your intuition, your true 'inner voice'. You can hear it to the extent that you give it your attention.
Martha Beck

Number Three

Miracles don't necessarily come with a clap of thunder or a flash of lightning... sometimes they come on tippy-toe.

Often people say, oh you're lucky, miracles always happen to *you* but no miracles ever happen in *my* life. Why do you think people say that? Often it is because they have this preconceived notion that miracles need to be a massive event like a clap of thunder or a lightning strike or winning five million dollars in a lottery. They think that there has to be something huge or amazing about it. They don't see that all sorts of small miracles are happening daily and are coming on quiet tippy toes so we don't see them or recognize them as easily.

A miracle is a wonder or a marvel, whether big or small. Simply, I believe it is a positive outflow of helpful energy. So, big or small, watch out for miracles everywhere. Be happy and gracious and receive them gratefully, no matter what the size.

Let me share a story with you. In 1985 we became instant parents. Judy and I had been married for eighteen years and had had no children, and we were philosophical about that. We had a very busy and happy life, both of us practicing chiropractic, speaking overseas usually once or twice a year, having a great time. A Canadian chiropractor friend, Dot, came to our home for Christmas in 1984 and she said that she and her husband were in the process of adopting a baby from Chile. Judy and I said, in typically forthright fashion, why would you want to do that? Like us you travel and have a great life, you have a wonderful profession you love, why would you want to give all that up? By the time Dot left at the start of the New Year, we looked at each other and just 'knew' that there were children waiting for us to find them.

Next morning Judy phoned the Department of Children's Services in Brisbane and was told quite bluntly that we were too old to adopt, that it was simply not possible. So now what? We live by 'never say never'. A clap of thunder miracle arrived. Dot told us of a man in Melbourne who was helping people gain guardianship of children in Chile and bringing them into Australia to formally adopt them, through a totally legal loop hole in the law in the state of Victoria.

This man was immensely helpful. In every state outside of Victoria, to adopt a child it was necessary to go through the Department of Children's Services, or the equivalent in your state, to get a letter of permission to adopt, for example, a boy or a girl, three years or two years old, or a baby. In Victoria, this letter was not absolutely necessary.

We put the process into motion. In Queensland we went through the same rigorous process all adoptive parents go through, with sociologist's reports about our suitability, a very detailed Home Study Report, a police check etc. Then everything had to be translated into Spanish. A tippy toe miracle was that the sociologist we found had previously worked for the department and knew precisely what was needed, as the department wasn't about to tell us or help us. We did everything by the book, everything that the authorities in Chile would require for this process to be approved.

Our new friend in Victoria, Graeme Orr, kindly gave us all the information we needed. We proceeded to contact some lawyers in Chile who worked with judges to allow children to be accessed. We were phoned in Australia at all hours of the night, and asked if we wanted this child or that child. Twin girls six months of age? No, absolutely not said Judy, horrified. When we heard boy, five years and girl three years, siblings, we were on the next plane.

Tippy toes or lightening flash? Those children weren't available. With a judge's help in Conception we found *our* boys, seven and a half and nearly nine. They were bigger boys, electively mute, but they were beautiful, sweet and sad boys from the country, recently arrived at the orphanage, and they were ours. When we saw them, that was it. Judy and I just couldn't believe the joy and love that overwhelmed us. We knew we had found our family.

To complete the process we trekked to a Judge in another part of the country where the children were from. This was like going to the outback in Australia. Outside the Court there was a long queue out into the street, as the Judge handled all different sorts of matters, criminal, civil and family. Our Spanish was so limited that we went inside to check we were in the right place and, tippy toes again, the Judge not only spoke English, but his hobby was Australian history! He had some gaps in his information about Australia so we did our best to complete stories of treks for him. This kind man did everything possible to support us to move forward. We didn't have a lawyer, we were doing it ourselves but we did need legal advice for the formalities. The Judge's assistant found a lawyer in the queue and he acted for us in exchange for moving his matter to the head of the queue.

"But," said the Judge, "There is a problem. These two beautiful boys have a sister that they have not seen for four and a half years. She has been in an orphanage in another part of the country. She is ten and a half years old and if you adopt the boys, you have to adopt her as well as we don't want to split the family. "We were so torn.

We felt we couldn't make a difference in that child's life. She had virtually no schooling, was hugely traumatized; the few years we would have to influence her wouldn't likely help. The boys hadn't mentioned her, and the boys would need a lot of care. We said no. After a lot of discussion with the Judge, he agreed that we could adopt the boys without their sister.

We left papers for a small girl with lawyers in Santiago for when we had settled the boys back home in Australia. Yes, we did think about the sister a lot. A lot. After a couple of weeks, Ignacio, our older son, went bright red from the top of his head to his toes when we asked him if he would like her to come to live with us. Lightning flash. Enough; we called Chile and started the process of adopting her. That's another story.

When we took the boys to the Australian Embassy in Santiago, we didn't have that letter saying we had permission to adopt in Queensland. Because we had all of our documentation in order in Chile and all exit documents were prepared, and everything was ready to go, we approached the Immigration Officer at the Australian Embassy, ready for a large miracle.

Australia, as a democracy lets us live where we want. We moved our address to Victoria one day before we left the country and we took up residence in Victoria with a sister of Judy's. We had taken an option to buy a practice in Victoria and we were returning to Victoria. That meant because of the Victorian connection, we didn't need the letter and it was up to the Immigration Officer to decide. She thought we were good people, we were giving these children a good home, we were professionals with income sufficient to pay for the special needs of the children, the paper work was impeccable. She did grant the entry visa. Because the sister was joining her brothers that visa was granted also when the attorney took our daughter to the Embassy several weeks later.

The first thing Shavela did when she came into our home on her arrival in Australia from Chile was have her ecstatic brothers show her where the pantry was. She examined its contents happily. Then she checked the fridge. She checked to make sure there was a machine that washed the clothes because she had had to wash clothes for the little children in the orphanage for years by hand. She matter of factly saw that there was a machine to dry the clothes and another one that washed the dishes. She had discovered these amazing machines for cloths and dishes when she stayed with our lawyer in Santiago for ten days prior to leaving Chile to fly to Australia. Then she wanted to eat.

Shavela was a tippy toe miracle. She came to us to be the mother to her brothers, as we found out years later. We all had to get used to one another and that took time. Shavela wasn't what we were expecting initially and we were really difficult for her for sure as we endeavoured to socialize her into Australian values and our way of life. What did evolve and tippy toe up to us was a sense of belonging to our complete family and having a richer and more wonderful life. These three amazing 'children', now in their mid-30s, are living lovely lives. Our sons have their own businesses and we have five healthy and gorgeous grandsons we are nuts about. Miracles abound.

Imagine if we had ignored our intuition to adopt.

We expected a miracle, and we received a massive miracle. So, go print some Expect A Miracle cards free from www.expectamiracle.com.au and start handing them out. Write down three or more miracles that happened to-day and no matter how tired you are write them down. Reflect back so the tippy toe ones that came your way. Why? They bring more to us because we recognize them!

Read your goals three times a day and read at least a story a day from the You Can Expect A Miracle books. Visit the website to make sure you live with this helpful mind set. Take your action steps and watch the miracles flow in.

Miracle 🗝 Four

Look for the miracles around you ... a bird on the wing, the beauty of a rose, the smile of a child. When you see the miracles that already exist, new ones arrive.

GOAL

GRATITUDE
Say
THANK YOU

TAKE
the
ACTION STEPS

CELEBRATE
the
"MIRACLE"

When you really consider the everyday things around you, they start to seem like tiny miracles.

Amy Shea

Number Four

Look for the miracles around you... a bird on the wing, the beauty of a rose, the smile of a child. When you see the miracles that already exist, new ones arrive.

There are so many miracle things that happen in our lives on a daily basis if we are open to seeing them and if we're looking for them. So many people are wearing blinkers. They can't see the good things out in front and around them. Their level of observation of beautiful things is not really open; they have shut down.

I'll share a story with you, about a man in his sixties who had everything. This man was a major international car executive. He was a pioneer in a big plant. He had a life that most people would have thought was amazing with numerous properties, all the toys you could possibly want in life, and all the money that such a privileged life could bring.

Judy and I had been speaking in the United States and we were coming home. Flying from the USA to Australia, the planes often arrive in Australia early in the morning after curfew has been lifted, so that means they leave Los Angeles from about 11.30pm till about 1.30am. To catch our flight, we were in Los Angeles International Airport in the Bradley building. There is a food court area on the upper floor and the only cafe or eatery of any sort that was open at midnight on this particular day was a Mexican Cafeteria with a server and a cashier out front. When the server produced the meals I put my hand into my pocket , as I do, and I pulled out my card holder. It is a beautiful George Jensen stainless steel creation, that feels so good when I hand out Expect A Miracle cards to people from it, I feel that I really value the card and the person.

II handed the server a card. As he took it, I gave my greeting "a gift for you". He took the card and he looked at it, turned it over to its blank side and he said "senor a miracle, senor, thank you senor, thank you!". Here we were at midnight, here was this tiny, very tired and elderly Mexican man absolutely thrilled with the gift of a card. He looked tongue tied, but he immediately sparked up and became more alive. He joyfully moved round the counter to show the cashier who said "what is expecting miracle?" By that time I was around the counter as well, and I put my hand in my pocket and said "for *you* senor, a card". "Senor, expect a miracle, me, oh senor I can get a miracle in my life, my life will change senor? Oh senior thank you, thank you for this miracle."

There was so much noise going on that the two cooks come out from the back. "What's this expect a miracle, what's this, what's this?". I said "would you like a card?" "si senor,si si si si!". II handed a card out to the other two , and the four of them were there looking at their cards, rejoicing about the miracles that could happen in their lives, about the possibilities awaiting them. They absolutely knew that just by having that card that miracles were coming. I was like a messenger in their minds.

Judy and I have often thought that with the synergy of like minds working together, that one plus one equal eleven not two. The synergy these four Mexican men were producing was electrifying.

There was a gentle "excuse me" that came from behind me, then a tap on the shoulder. A man said "sir would you have a spare one of those cards"? "Yes sure, certainly, here is a card for you sir". I turned around and heard "are you eating with anybody else", I replied "with my wife and please join us". When we had our dinner and were sitting with Judy he told us that his field was change management. This person obviously was a highly respected professional in the work he did, because when a major company was absolutely stuck in business, he went in to help solve problems and refocus them. He said he trained numerous people, had consultant companies, and now in his retirement he was called in to assist with jobs that absolutely needed a trouble shooter, the top gun – my words, not his. He was very self effacing, actually.

He said "I have not seen energy like that in people in years. These people would be living week to week quite likely and on very little, but they were delighted and so grateful to have the card and its message. They could see that their life could change" Smiling broadly he concluded. "All I can do is say thank you. Meeting you has been amazing for my life." I assured him that the card was a life changer for so many.

We parted, exchanging regular business cards. Judy and I went to catch our flight; he went off to catch his. A few days later I received an email from the businessman. He told us that his wife had left him after thirty five years of marriage a couple of weeks before and he was just blown away. He hadn't suspected a thing. He had agreed to do a job for a major corporation and didn't like to let people down. He said he had just completed his obligation and had met us as he was on his way home to commit suicide.

He explained "I saw enormous transformational energy produced from those three words, Expect A Miracle, that you gave those people. I saw what it did to change their thought pattern."

He continued," I thought that I, too, can expect a miracle to find another woman to have in my life to share the beautiful things I have and to share happiness with me. I arrived home and I dismantled the suicide apparatus I had prepared in another car parked in my garage. I'm a changed man. It amazes me that it was so simple. It was a simple thing and a small thing. It was a thought, it was an idea, that moved the Mexicans forward and it has now changed my life."

Our new friend knew that he had to take action steps to change his life, which were to dismantle the gear, celebrate newly found acceptance and hope, and give gratitude, so he could move on to his new life.

Be on the lookout for all the beautiful things, even small things that cross our path each day. We have five grandchildren now and the first time I saw each of those grandchildren smile, it was heart stopping, and I could so easily not have taken the time to be present for those moments. When we first found our boys in the orphanage in Chile they almost didn't speak, and we knew really almost zero Spanish. We told them and whispered in their ears day and night, "I love you, I love you, I love you". Rod our youngest son was the first to say any words in English and he had learnt those words well "I love you".

If we do something, anything positive, no matter how small it is, it can produce great results. My mission in life is to continue to hand out Expect A Miracle cards. You can print cards off for yourself from my website. I suggest you write down your miracles, no matter how small and how tiny they are, in your diary or in your journal every day. Go to the website to read a great story of beautiful things before you go to sleep, or go to one of the You Can Expect A Miracle books and read a story. When you do that it's an attraction tool to bring wonders or marvels your way and you will become a *miracle maker* and a *miracle magnet.*

Miracle 🔑 Five

Go with the flow ... sometimes at first sight the miracles we get don't appear to be the ones we want.

GOAL

TAKE
the
ACTION STEPS

GRATITUDE
Say
THANK YOU

CELEBRATE
the
"MIRACLE"

Change is not a bolt of lightning that arrives with a zap. It is a bridge built brick by brick, every day, with sweat and humility and slips. It is hard work, and slow work, but it can be thrilling to watch it take shape.

Sarah Hepola

Number Five

Go with the flow ... sometimes at first sight the miracles we get don't appear to be the ones we want.

Sometimes when we go out in the world looking for or expecting or hoping for something, and we're really focused on getting a particular outcome or miracle, that's not what we receive at that time.

It's so   important that when any miracles come, that we receive them and say "thank you!" even if they're not the ones we're expecting or wanting. If we're not grateful and receive them happily when they do come, our miracle mind-set can become jaded and faded. We don't recognize other miracles coming to us. The world can look a harsher place.

A story I'll relate to you is a funny story – it was hysterical when it happened. This story was set in 1970. Judy and I had moved from Denmark where we'd been living and working to Great Britain and Ireland to travel in our tiny Volkswagen Beetle, and camp along the way in our tent.

It was almost five o'clock in the afternoon, on a soft evening in County Cork, Ireland and we'd been travelling all day. We had been cruising down beautiful country lanes, eyes feasting on emerald greens, those beautiful Irish greens. We came around a corner and saw a glorious view of rolling hills, stone fences, tall forests and lush fields, a breathtaking view, complete with a weather beaten farmer leaning on a gate. Rapidly we stopped, and we said, "Sir, we do need somewhere to camp tonight, would it be possible for us to pitch our tent in this paddock?"

The farmer was approaching sixty years of age. He had farmed the family acres all his life, living in a traditional thatched roof cottage farm house, basic but beautiful. And he replied, "Hah! I be wondering would you be staying here for a week, would you? Oh my golly, this is such a beautiful place you'd be wanting to be staying here. You'd have to stay here for a week." I said, "No, but thanks a million, we don't have that time available." "You'll need to be staying at least two nights. Two nights you should be staying, because tonight it's the bingo, and my wife will have to take you to the Bingo as guests of her. Tomorrow night it's the singing pub, and I can take you and her to the singing pub and I'll just be moving the bull out of this paddock". We said thanks you, that would all be wonderful.

We were putting our little tent up and the farmer came back and said, "You'd be wanting some milk, would you? Yes indeedy, straight from the cow. Oh here's some fresh milk, and you like the cream too?" We thanked him and were handed a big billycan of milk, a big pat of fresh butter, and thick cream. Next he said "Would you be liking the mushrooms?" We said we love mushrooms. He came back later with a four gallon tin full of fresh mushrooms and was so, so helpful and friendly. He invited us to come and meet the children and his Mrs. We followed him to the cottage and met his wife, half his age, a beautiful shy woman with two children peeking out from around her skirt... lovely country folk. "And the wife will be taking you to the bingo tonight", our farmer said.

We went on foot to the bingo in a massive church hall, big enough for a major city. Five hundred people played bingo...unbelievable. The wife didn't play as she was one of those who sold and handed out the bingo cards out. It was very cheap to play a card and if you won the bingo, you won maybe ten pounds.

We happened to be there on a very special night. On the last game there was a jackpot that had been going on and accumulating for months. This jackpot was five hundred Irish pounds. Teaching positions that we were soon to take up in London paid twenty five pounds a week. That was to be our weekly income. Five hundred pounds was a big sum for us. We were camping in farmer's fields and on the sides of roads, buying cheap but fresh foods in markets. It allowed us to travel very, very cheaply in those days for many weeks. So, wow this was huge, this bingo prize, this five hundred pounds.

Guess who won that, ME! I yelled, "BINGO!" and wow, the house went nuts. Well the farmer's wife was delighted because her guest had won. Who came to give away the prize money? The Monsignor of the parish, dressed in all his finery, gown to the floor, official hat on; this was a big event. He was dressed as if he was about to have an audience with the Pope. He came up to us and he had my winnings, the five hundred pounds in fifty pound notes, fanned out on a plate.

Well, this was our miracle. Imagine how many weeks, nay months we could travel on that money. Five hundred pounds! He nodded his head and said, "I hear you're a guest here from Australia, my boy. Welcome to Ireland ... oh it's so good to have you here. I can just see in your face and your eyes my boy; you're a very, very kind man. You're a *very* kind man. And it's so wonderful that you could win this Bingo Jackpot tonight. This winning pot has been building for weeks, and weeks and weeks. Everybody has wanted to win this. I know you're such a kind man my boy, and Australians are known as kind people, kind people indeed. So, I know that you'd be happy to give this fifty pounds here to the church for the restoration fund, and I know this fifty pounds here you'd be very happy to give to the roof replacement fund, and this fifty pounds for the missionaries in Africa, and this fifty pounds here to...". On and on he went until there was one solitary fifty pound note left on the plate. "And everyone let's stand up and give this boy from Australia a big clap and a big cheer for being such a kind and generous man, for looking after the parish. Here's your fifty pounds. Congratulations and may God bless you with that me boy."

Wow, this man, this Monsignor was fantastic. Here was my miracle man, my five hundred pounds literally on a plate and he proceeded to remove four hundred and fifty pounds very easily, very simply, very quickly and he had everyone cheer. I still had a miracle, fifty pounds... which was great, albeit smaller than I originally thought. He was a miracle worker. He had his miracle, that he kept four hundred and fifty pounds for the church. Another miracle for me was seeing someone with such skill in action and someone who used everything for the greater good. He put it out there and he made it happen.

It wasn't quite the miracle that had been possible for me, but I knew I was receiving something else that was amazingly valuable. We just had a most beautiful experience with Irish folk who we would never otherwise have met. We had a wonderful time. We went to sing in the pub and Judy sat in the coveted place, on the warm bricks at the fire side. Just us and the locals welcomed us fully. People came to thank me, sincerely, and we shared a few chuckles at how smooth the Monsignor had been at my expense, with 'and let me buy you a beer, my boy'.

This was before my days of Expect A Miracle cards, but now if something like that happened, I would make sure that I would have plenty ready to give away to thank the people.

I urge you to watch for miracles that aren't what you have expected or asked for. Yes, we do have to have goals and work towards them but great things can come to us in *unexpected packages* that are gifts none the less.

To create more miracles in your life, you could write down three or more wins, wins small, medium and large in your diary or journal each day. Read a story, a beautiful story that sends you off to bed ready for miracles next day. Go to the website to read some great stories. Please post miracle stories to inspire others.

Remember the formula for creating miracles; set the goal, take the action steps, celebrate the miracle and give thanks and gratitude back to the source for whatever arrives. Remember, as Judy says, a miracle is a wonder or a marvel, big or small, created by an outpouring of positive energy.

Miracle Six

It's okay to ask ... miracles are for everyone, we all deserve them.

GOAL

GRATITUDE
Say
THANK YOU

TAKE
the
ACTION STEPS

CELEBRATE
the
"MIRACLE"

Asking is the beginning of receiving. Make sure you don't go to the ocean with a teaspoon. At least take a bucket so the kids won't laugh at you.

Jim Rohn

Number Six

It's okay to ask... miracles are for everyone, we all deserve them.

I am privileged to be asked to speak to chiropractic students on inspirational topics at various institutions around the world from time to time and recently I was in Melbourne, Australia at RMIT University. I went out to dinner prior to my presentation with the President of the Student Association to an illustrious Italian restaurant.

I asked the waiter for steamed vegetables with my stuffed pasta instead of salad and was told, "No, it's not possible". I said I was happy to pay extra, but still, "no, that's not possible". In a situation like this I love to explore different perspectives with an individual who is 'stuck' in a particular paradigm and lacks flexibility. I gave the waiter one of my *Expect A Miracle* cards, saying "a gift for you". His face was a picture of a smile, of understanding and of 'sure, I'll give it a go', and I said, "Here's a card for the chef. Can you please give it to him from me?" A bigger smile now filled my waiters face, he was positively beaming.

Our waiter was a busy fellow and as he was moving off to his next task I said, "Before you go, do you actually serve steamed vegetables here?" The waiter said, "oh yes, we have steamed vegetables, but they only come with meat dishes". My next question was, "isn't my pasta stuffed with minced veal?" His answer was, "yes, sir". My next question was, "isn't that meat?"

He came back rapidly and said you can have your steamed vegetables sir. He shared with me that this had never happened at the restaurant before. "It is amazing; our team of waiters can't believe it. Here we only serve garden salad or rocket salad with pasta dishes". I said to my student host, "a funny thing is that when you ask, it's amazing what happens. The person can either say yes, or the person can say no, but you can ask again a little differently. They might say no again, but miracles can happen."

Young kids are great at creating miracles. How often does a child ask you for something? They'll ask, and they'll ask, and they'll ask, and they'll hear your no, no, no, until they catch you in a desperate moment and it has to be a yes. We can try to hide our caving in with conditions, but they will still often attempt to find another way of securing a *YES* answer. As we grow up, the asking skill can be knocked out of us with all the no's we hear, especially if the people delivering them are cross. I suggest that you start asking again and see what miracles you can bring into your life, large and small.

I'll share a story with you. In 1980, we sold our practice in Foster, New South Wales and moved to Brisbane in the neighbouring state of Queensland. After checking out a number of areas we found a beautiful home we wanted to buy. We had a quarter of the price as down payment. I went to the head office of our bank in Brisbane with a letter from our Bank Manager in Foster introducing us as very good solid customers. Judy and I had come back to Australia after travelling and studying overseas for ten years. Starting with no money on our return to Australia we had set up two chiropractic practices and we had done very well financially in eighteen months. However, the bank thought our track record hadn't been for long enough and we would be starting again in Brisbane, in the city and not a small country town, and also another state. In the bank's wisdom, they said no.

We had signed a cash thirty day contract as we believed we would have no trouble securing the mortgage. I asked our solicitor if he knew anywhere else we could go to secure the loan, perhaps even another bank. Our solicitor said, "No worries, I know just the bank manager who will give you the loan you are seeking, I'll call him right now". As our solicitor predicted the bank manager took down our personal details and the property details and gave us an approval immediately over the phone. We were novices in the property world at that time only ever having purchased a home in Canada and then our first Australian home in Forster some two years earlier.

Our solicitor said it's a twenty minute walk from here to the bank so take your time as Ron Smith (we will call him) our new bank manager is having the documentation prepared now so it will be ready when you arrive. I was so excited and happy on receiving the yes answer that I felt like I was floating along as I made my way to a new part of the city I had never seen before.

I'm talking 1980, pre computer days. Today a twenty year old can sit at a computer somewhere in another state, across the other side of the country, and make the decisions about who can borrow and who cannot based on algorithms. The decisions in those days were made by the bank manager himself based on his personal lending limit which may have been several hundred thousand dollars up to several million dollars.

The strange thing was that on this day our new solicitor had arranged the loan for us at a small city branch of the same bank that the Head Office lenders had refused our application several hours earlier.

I was sitting waiting in somewhat an anxious state when the door opened from the manager's office with a flurry. Out came this fellow who was in his fifties, balding, welcoming and naturally engaging with a big smile on his face. He looked like he played in the front row of a rugby scrum; he was big and chunky. He thrust his hand out and said, "Johnny Hinwood is that right? I'm Ron Smith, the manager here, come into my office my boy".

He ushered me into his sparsely furnished office, offered me a seat and went onto say, "I understand that you've got twenty thousand bickies, the property is eighty thousand bickies and you need sixty thousand bickies, that's right, isn't it?" I replied, "Absolutely". He went on, "well I can lend you the forty thousand bickies and I've already called the boys around the corner at the banks sister finance company and they have the remainder of your finance organized. They're drawing up the documents right now for a second mortgage of ten thousand bickies, so we've got it all taken care of my boy. You've got the twenty bickies, I'm providing the sixty bickies and you get the property. It's that easy?"

Never before had I met a bank manager who was so cool and with it. I shook his hand and said, "I don't know we can ever thank you enough for helping us purchase our home". Ron Smith replied, "Yes, it can be that easy my boy, remember, all you have to do is ask for what you really want in life".

I had a big learning that day. Keep knocking on the closed door, maybe someone will answer you and you'll get a yes response.

Most people don't ask, or they are put off because someone said no. This guy was an amazing bank manager and we stayed with him for many years. He was such a genuine human being. He was one of those people called 'the fix it man'. He would be moved by Head Office into bank branches that were not doing well, where the manager was hopeless and the customers were leaving. Ron Smith would do a remarkable recovery job of the branch and of course he had customers who would follow him from other branches like us where he had weaved his magic to support us. We referred many new customers to Ron.

There were some members of the middle order management in the banking group who were very jealous of Ron's high level of success where ever he was sent to get a branch out of its downhill slide. Ron unfortunately had one customer, a developer who was caught out and defaulted on a large loan. This mistake was enough for this small group of placement officers to massively downgrade Ron and punish him for his mistake.

He was put in charge of Credit Card Bad Debts. He was given a very small staff and the task of recovering money from people who went over on their credit card limit, often young women especially, who couldn't afford to pay. It was too costly for the bank to bankrupt them and the debts were just written off.

Ron arrived on the scene, he devised a recovery plan, he briefed his staff, he laid out his plan and he trained his support team. He would personally demonstrate how easy it was to collect bad debts. He would phone someone who owed say five hundred dollars and say, "Good day darling! This is Ron Smith, and I'm in charge of the credit card help unit. I see you've got into a bit of trouble. We all sometimes get into a little bit of financial trouble, I understand, the bank understands.

So what I'm going to do is this; I'll re-open your credit card account again, and I want to give you a hundred dollars to treat and pamper yourself. Get some nice perfume or a new dress so you feel really, really good. What I want you to do is come to an agreement with me that you will pay this debt off at $30 a week or $50 a week". He came up with an agreed payment plan with each of these people and they started paying and kept their agreements in almost all cases. This was miracle stuff.

I was staggered. He recovered millions of dollars in bad debts that had been written off by the bank. He created miracles for the bank but also for lots of people who were in real trouble, offering a helping hand and asking if they wanted a way out so they could move forward with grace and feeling honourable in their lives. His superiors, who believed Ron Smith would finally fail, were yet again proven wrong. They had to get him out of this position as he was recovering all sorts of money that had already been written off and the accounting boffin's didn't know how handle the income. It was all too hard.

Ron returned to branch banking and left the bank soon after with forty years of service behind him as he just couldn't handle the bureaucracy anymore.

He purchased a very run down motel and in months it was a thriving cash cow business.

Ron Smith was a beautiful man who understood the science of asking and also of giving and receiving. The more we ask, the more miracles we attract into our lives.

Make sure you go and print some *Expect A Miracle* cards off the website and start handing them out, giving them to people as gifts. When we have unconditionally given people those gifts, often people have said 'Thank you", and asked us what they can do for us. We ask for nothing in return, but sometimes unsolicited and unexpected miracles come back to us.

Judy and I have had amazing upgrades of rental cars and of hotel rooms especially. I remember going to speak in Mallorca, Spain, and we arrived at our beautiful stately hotel on the harbor front in Palma at about one in the morning. Our bags had been lost in transit somewhere between Australia and Spain. We gave the night manager and his assistant an *Expect A Miracle* card each and they were over the moon. He asked us if we had any more cards, so we gave him as many as many as he wanted. At breakfast the next morning all the staff had an *Expect A Miracle* card under their name tag. It was fantastic to see.

We went across to the other side of the island a couple of days later to speak at our conference. When we arrived back at our beautiful Palma hotel for a week's holiday the manager was waiting to welcome us and we were given status lie we were royalty. We received all sorts of complimentary goodies we were given the Presidential Suite. Our suite looked out over the magnificent harbor. We could have had two hundred people party on our private terrace and we were graced with every courtesy possible.

The staff was all so grateful for their *Expect A Miracle* cards. They loved them. We loved sharing the gift of sharing the *Expect A Miracle* cards and surely were grateful for our miracle suite and all the goodies we received.

Please write down three miracles each day that happen in your life, no matter how small they are. Remember a miracle is something of wonder; it's a marvel, big or small, an out flowing of positive energy. Go through your goals every day, and remember that a great place to keep your goals is on the back of *Expect A Miracle* cards. Read your goals at least once daily, read at least one miracle story a day from one of the You Can Expect A Miracle books or from the website. Be daring go and post stories on the website that you have written to inspire and help others.

To create more miracles, remember the cycle; set the goal, create the action steps, take action, celebrate the miracles, "wohooo", and give gratitude. Say thank you.

Miracle 🗝 Seven

If you have the courage to persist in going for what you really want in life, you will often get it.

GOAL

GRATITUDE
Say
THANK YOU

TAKE
the
ACTION STEPS

CELEBRATE
the
"MIRACLE"

Before you can ask for anything you have to know what you want and you have to believe that it is possible for you to get it.

Jack Canfield & Mark Victor Hansen

Number Seven

If you have the courage to persist in going for what you really want in life, you will usually get it.

If we ask for something we want in life, we can receive two responses, yes or no. Easy. What's to fear? If it is a no, it's not usually personal – ask someone else or ask differently. If you 'go there' and are courageous and ask, the positive outcome will so often surprise you. YES, can happen! It's amazing what people are willing to do and to give you and how they will support you, love you and care for you when you ask.

If you go out and ask *and* you're excited and enthusiastic as well, the extraordinary can happen. Enthusiasm surely makes the difference. Enthusiasm is the tool that can open the door that's stuck. It releases energy to bring things into life. The most enthusiastic person I've met, next to our great late mentor, Charlie "Tremendous" Jones, was Charlie's long time friend, the enigmatic Norman Vincent Peale.

Dr Norman Vincent Peale was a famous preacher from New York. He was a short stocky man, a bundle of energy and so well known for his landmark book, *The Power of Positive Thinking.* When he was eighty four years old he was on an Australian speaking tour with our friend 'Tremendous' Jones and Charlie had been telling him about our three beautiful children we had adopted from Chile eighteen months earlier. When they were speaking in Brisbane in 1987 Charlie organized for Dr and Mrs Peale to meet us and our children Shavela, Ignacio and Rodrigo for breakfast.

Picture this - a couple of hundred people in the dining room of a five star classy hotel, the place is full and noisy with breakfast diners and never ending chatter. Norman Vincent Peale had a very distinctive voice, a big voice, honed by overcoming dodgy sound systems for over sixty years of his speaking career. When I say he had a piercing voice, it was. It was a voice that had incredible authority and presence behind it and all one wanted to do was listen to this magnetic voice when he spoke. He was seated opposite to me at the table.

After we had all served ourselves from the buffet we sat down and engaged in typical meet and greet conversation. All of a sudden Dr Peale moved into a state of deep engagement with me across the table and his face took on a very inquiring look. He then stood up, and came around the end of the table to stand beside me. My mind was in wonderment at what was coming next. He bent forward so he had direct eye to eye contact with me and said, "John! Do you have any problems in your life my boy?!" I looked at him and said, "Dr, Peale, I do have some problems." He said, "Oh... I'm glad my boy! cause I'm gonna be praying to the good Lord right now for you John!"

All of a sudden in that noisy dining room you could have heard a pin drop. Everybody was totally tuned into what was coming next from this human dynamo. "Lord... Give John problems! Give John big problems!, Give John more problems!, Give John lots of problems!" It was riveting listening, I guess, someone wishing a family man even more problems! Unabashed, the Dr carried on, hugely focused. "John, if you are a man who hasn't got problems, *you ain't growing* my boy. I can see you adopted these children so you're a growing couple, and I pray to the Lord to give you problems! More problems!"

I could feel all the patrons in the restaurant at that moment were focused on the two of us. It was an incredible deep down feeling of being totally in the spotlight. In the middle of instant parenthood, Judy and I looked at one another askance, but the message was so very powerful and extremely useful. Problems are how we grow, so embrace them and welcome them, and *ASK*, loudly with enthusiasm for help and assistance if you feel you need it.

We finished our breakfast and we all had big hugs with the Peals' and "Tremendous" before taking the kids off to their ESL (English as a Second Language) school. I don't think the kids really understood too much of what went on that morning, however everyone else in the restaurant surely did.

In Hawaii, back in the early nineteen nineties, we were doing a ten day Global Educators training program with Robert Kiyosaki. In those days Robert was not a famous author, sought after keynote speaker or talk show guest, he was a fierce seminar and workshop facilitator. His many books followed several years later. This program had about a hundred and fifty people participating over ten days. The essence of the program was how you handled mental, emotional, spiritual and physical stuff in your life and understanding why you were not succeeding when you hit one or more of these road blocks that you could not handle.

Robert especially loved the physical stuff. He said that this area of our lives when we are cornered and have to win, our true behaviour is revealed. Games are a true reflection of our behaviour.

We were randomly divided up by a numbering system into teams of eight people. Once we were all in our teams, Robert announced we were about to start a volleyball tournament. We played a knockout competition starting day one in the afternoon through till we got to the last day, and the morning of the last day was the final. Some of the teams, that came out through this random numbering process were awesome on paper and how they physically looked.

They were some teams of all young men who thought they were hot. Young bucks who worked in the share trading 'boiler rooms' and would do anything to win! They were into the win/lose mentality, and they had a mindset of winning BIG at whatever they participated in. These highly athletic guys who would strut the gym daily were all of a sudden actively competing in an athletic team event with team members they didn't know. These teams I am referring to looked to the naked eye as teams of champions.

The team of eight that I was drafted into was made up of two men and six women. At this point in my life I was fast approaching fifty, I was very fit, ran every day, had played competitive sport all my life, and my initial career was as a physical education teacher. I was not in the league athletically of the 'hot shot young bucks' who were already predicting that they were the hot favourites to win the tournament and the grand cash prize. The other man in our team was in his forties and a book worm. He had never really played sport, not even in school.

Now to the six women... five were Asian from Singapore, who had never participated in sports in their life. The sixth woman in that group was an Aussie who had played lots of sport. So we had two people out of eight who'd ever played sport, even at school level.

Volleyball has simple rules. Two teams on a court about the size of a tennis court with a net height for our competition of about 2.30 meters or 7 feet 6 inches. The ball a bit smaller than a soccer ball is batted by each team to and fro over the net until one team either bats it out of bounds or into the net. To make the game more interesting and set up tactical situations each team may bat the ball between themselves in their court area up to three times before it has to pass over the net to their opposing team.

For our team of raw novices, just getting the ball over the net by the server was going to be a *HUGE* task. Another rule in volleyball is that each team member must rotate and be the server and they then serve until they lose a point.

So here we are at a Robert Kiyosaki live in ten day event and to up the commitment level Robert tells you that each player has to put a slab of money on the table so their team can participate in the event. It was two thousand four hundred dollars per team fee or three hundred dollars for each team member. In the end, whoever won the final, pocketed the lot.

If the bookmakers had been giving odds on who would win based on the makeup of the teams and their team members, we would have been the longest odds at 1,000 to 1. As does happen from time to time the rank outsider gets up and wins the event against all odds.

So how did we win? What happened, what was the miracle here? The miracle was that each member of our team decided that we would be a championship team, and not a team of champions. We sat down and brainstormed how we could support each other and what we needed to do to prepare for our first game. We had no 'jocks' in the team, little in the way of athletic skills by most of our team members, but we all had big hearts and persistence and we decided to totally support each other, no matter what.

As I was the most experienced and had taught high school kids how to play volleyball, the team asked me would I be the captain and coach them also. I said absolutely as long as Robyn my Aussie team mate who had played lots of sport would be the vice captain my assistant coach. The Miracle Team was born. Our other six team members were all highly successful business people in their own right, so succeeding at a non contact sport where team work was paramount was an easy concept to accept, especially when no one had an ego they had to parade.

We spent all of our free time in the breaks practicing the skills of batting the ball, digging it out when it was close to the ground and serving. We didn't sit around like most of the other attendees in the breaks who were generally just 'shooting the breeze'. As the seminar venue was at a big hotel at Kona on the Big Island in Hawaii our games were played on the beach, so diving for balls on sand was an easy task and there was little chance of personal injury.

Most of the other groups didn't bother to practice and were happy that they would just turn up for their matches and get it together on the court. Not the Miracle Team. Robyn and I were continually asking our fellow team members, "how can we help you?" and these total virgins to volleyball kept asking questions and they were so eager to learn and they had no fear of making mistakes. Our mantra was... practice, practice, practice, practice... and we did just that.

Everybody understood that the server had to get the ball over the net as high as possible into the back of the opponent's court so it could not be blocked by our opponents and smashed back. Consistency in our serving was the key. No fancy stuff, that was easy for our team as almost all of our team members didn't understand what fancy volleyball stuff was anyway.

The tournament started and one the early casualties was the 'super all male jock's team'. It was a classic case of a team of champions where egos were so big everyone was falling over them. No one trusted their other team members to get it right and the 'sharking' that happened with every play became laughable. The 'hot shot' serving went all wrong and team arguments broke out. If someone made a mistake, and there were plenty of them, they were castigated initially and lynching was fast approaching by the end of their game.

We played our very basic game of serve high and deep, get it in the court and then bat the ball back over the net deep into the court; no spiking or smashing on our team and only a little blocking. Our tactic was to wait for our opponents to make a mistake.

In the end the strategy worked and we went through and we won the tournament and the cash booty. The rank outsiders won the tournament. Everyone in our team participated at their very best level physically, mentally, emotional and spiritually. We set a team goal, we totally trusted each other and then took the action steps of practicing every spare moment we had and we left our egos in our rooms. Those in our team who had trouble serving we gave those heaps of supportive practice one on one. When we won a point, we celebrated it as a miracle. Woohoo! We were out there patting each other on the back, giving high fives, group hugs and whatever else our emotions created in the moment.

Interestingly the last thing was gratitude. We continually displayed gratitude to each other. Thank you, thank you. It was huge that everyone gave of their best in every moment.

When I agreed to take on the team coach and captain position I explained the saying... "A job worth doing is worth doing lousy." Fortunately everyone in our team ran with the concept immediately. It was very easy for us because when we started as 'The Miracle Team' we were lousy. There were teams who started who were very good, but we were lousy. However, every game we played, every practice we had, we got better, and better, and better till in the end it was a miracle, we expected it and we received it.

What did I do with my winnings of two thousand dollars? I decided to invest it in a keep sake to always remind me of how our team of also ran's became a championship Miracle Team. On returning to Honolulu for a few days' holiday and relaxation before returning home I purchased a beautiful Gucci watch which was exactly two thousand dollars. I wear that watch every time I speak now to remind me that if I concentrate on owning the basics and I deliver rock solid content then I will continue to experience miracles in my life.

Miracle 🗝 Eight

Find time to just sit and put your brain into freewheeling mode. Just let it run free ... busy brains sometimes miss miracles!

GOAL

TAKE
the
ACTION STEPS

GRATITUDE
Say
THANK YOU

CELEBRATE
the
"MIRACLE"

Stillness is where creativity and solutions to problems are found.

Eckhart Toll

Number Eight

Find time to just sit and put your brain into freewheeling mode. Just let it run free... busy brains sometimes miss miracles.

Some people are always *doing* things, they never take time out. When I finish my video session later today, I'll be going to the gym for my thirty minute workout and then I'll spend another twenty five minutes swimming forty laps or one kilometre in the pool. When I am exercising I just let my brain run free, and this is my version of meditation where I'm not thinking about anything at all. I let my mind empty and go where it will. It's amazing what comes to me at those times, thoughts that when I'm doing the busyness in my life, I must block out or I don't have time to allow these thoughts to come to the surface.

As strange as it may sound to some people, exercise for me is relaxing and my brain enjoys its opportunity to go into freewheeling mode.

In the middle of the night I sometimes wake briefly and jot down ideas that come to me when I'm sleeping. I keep a pocket sized note pad and pen on my side table. I also keep a pen and small pad in the car so when ideas come up I can take a moment to record them. If I'm not thinking about anything while driving in the car, other than just keeping safe and out of trouble, my brain can be in free-wheeling mode. If you're letting yourself roam and dream you can access what Albert Einstein refers to as the other ninety percent of your mind.

A friend sent me something on Face book a few weeks ago, and it was 'the one hundred places you need to visit in your life', with a score sheet. The average score for people who completed the questionnaire was eight out of a possible hundred places. I must admit the list was quite "USA centric". I did go through it and I scored seventy eight out of a hundred. Bragging? No – Judy and I love to see new places, meet interesting folks and explore new cultures. Some people do value travel, some people just don't.

Completing this 'one hundred places visited' score sheet I was prompted to find a map of the world. I discovered we've visited one hundred and nine countries. Many of these countries we had driven through when Judy and I were 'on the road' from 1969 through to 1973 as we wandered the world, often off the beaten track, before we started studying for our second career path in Canada. Mostly our travel was by public transport, other than in Africa where we bought a Land Rover four-wheel drive workhorse vehicle in England .We drove from London to South Africa, across the Sahara Desert, west, central and east Africa and on into southern Africa. We had many incredible miracle experiences and meeting such interesting people enriched out lives.

All this travel gave us a plenty of time to guarantee that free-wheeling mode time was available a-plenty. When in that free-wheeling mode, it was amazing the things that we were open to experience all around us which were often absolute miracles. There's one section of time, about a three-week period in central and east Africa that was quite astonishing, exceptionally interesting and miraculous at the same time.

We were hi-jacked in a very remote part of the Congo. The track was very narrow and confined on both sides by very thick jungle and it was very steamy. We had no air-conditioning in 1972 and the heat was quite over bearing. We were driving extremely slowly as we were squeezing past a massive, hugely overloaded Mercedes truck when I suddenly felt something pressed to my right forehead – sure enough, a gun - and a voice yelling loudly at me in French. The hijacker was clearly telling me to stop, get out and give him my truck. I didn't need to understand French to decipher his actions and intentions.

I must admit, I've never been good with someone telling me what to do with my stuff, especially at this time, as this was our home on wheels. In fact it was the only home we had and it contained all our worldly possessions. My immediate reaction was to tell the 'XYZ' in pretend army gear what I thought of him and his peashooter and that the only way he could ever have my Land Rover, was in his dreams. Judy was marvellous. She immediately burst into tears. In amazingly voluble and gesticulating schoolgirl French (later she told me she said something like this)..."I'm so sorry; this is a stupid, stupid man I am with. You can see how *stupid* he is. (As she hit my ribs with another massive elbow blow) How can we help you? Did I understand you – please excuse my very bad French – to say we can help you? And how could we do that? You need to go to a village? Of course we will take you. Don't take any notice of this stupid and bad man I am with. I see you are a good, brave man and you need help. Ah, but if we take *you* to the next village then who will look after your loaded truck and all the people you have on your truck? Perhaps you have a lieutenant who could come with us? Oh, I see, there is a prisoner as well, a murderer you say, (being held by a rope around his waist). Certainly we will take both men to the next army post".

Unexpectedly I heard a German voice in broken English come from way up on the top of the truck saying "I vould not argue with vis dis man, he has killed two men already dis morning". I must admit I suddenly wasn't quite as brave, and I shut up while Judy sorted out the details.

Yes, we did deliver the lieutenant and his prisoner to the next village a day later after lurching through a rutted track that wound its' way through the jungle. The prisoner bounced along in the stifling heat of the panelled back section of our vehicle, next to our knives and all manner of potential implements.

Oh, we love Africa! Somehow it's been in our 'bones' since we arrived there.

Only about a week after that we left the Congo and urged our vehicle into Uganda across and along ruts where the vehicle often was lost up to its' axles.

We suddenly had the urge to explore as far as we could in a northerly direction up the Nile River. There were few vehicles in this area in those days (1971), in the north of Uganda. We dawdled along basic dirt tracks for a couple of hours. Suddenly we arrived at a large waterfall in the course of the river. As we turned around the corner a big army truck was parked on a bridge over the river, its' canvas sides let down. Heavily drunk soldiers were lurching and they were doing something strange. As we edged closer it was apparent that bodies were being taken out of the truck and being thrown into the Albert Nile, to the crocodiles that we could plainly see were very receptive.

I'm so grateful we were still a distance away out of immediate reach and sight. I'm grateful that they hadn't expected us and that someone hadn't been on century duty with a gun at the ready. Instead, there were rifles up against the side of their body laden truck. I'm ever grateful for the alcoholic haze these men were in. They were gibbering and laughing as they threw body after body off the bridge and into the river. These soldiers were members of the President of Uganda, Idi Amin's genocide and execution squad.

Judy insisted that we fast go bush, off track for a few days. In dramatic contrast a few hours and many miles later we met some warm, friendly and welcoming people in a small remote village. Beautiful memories remain of a sweet sharing encounter we had with this small group of people who were waiting to be found eventually by the genocide squad.

Judy's alertness once again was a miracle life saver.

A couple of weeks later, I decided that I wanted to climb Mount Kilimanjaro when we arrived in Tanzania. Judy's Uncle Walter whom we met and spent time with when we lived and worked in London referred to 'Kili' on several occasions when we were walking with him and Aunt Lena on the Yorkshire moors. Walter was in his late seventies at that time and he had vivid memories of the stories his father had told him of his life in Africa as an officer in the British Army. 'Kili' then for me, became one of those things and one of those places that I placed on the 'bucket list' that lived in my brain.

There it was on the equator, magnificent, cloudless, snow capped, as we drove across the plains towards it. It just had to be climbed. Nineteen thousand three hundred and forty one feet, three days up and two days down was the journey time. The closer we drove towards this mountain of splendour the more I could feel adrenalin moving in my body and the urge to climb this peak.

My only other experience in life, climbing a high majestic mountain, was in January of 1964 when I was hitch hiking around New Zealand as an eighteen year old. As we approached the Egmont National Park in the Taranaki region on the west coast of New Zealand's North Island, the eight thousand two hundred and sixty one feet of the volcano Taranaki (or Mt Egmont as it is also known) rules supreme stood tall above the surrounding landscape. The snow capped peak in the middle of summer was something I had only ever seen on television, at the movies or in books.

At first sight I knew I just had to climb that mountain.

I arrived in New Plymouth at tea time on Saturday and found a cheap boarding house for the night. Over dinner that night, I met two young New Zealand SAS soldiers, who were on holiday and were in New Plymouth for the 'Climb Mt Egmont Open Day'. They invited me to join them the next day. I was stoked!

As we talked over dinner that night about how we would climb the Mount Taranaki or Mount Egmont the next day I learnt that it was an active but quiescent volcano that had last erupted in 1860. The three of us stayed up very late that night chatting about the adventure ahead. We had to rise at five the next morning as the climb from the car park started at six o'clock.

All three of us over slept the alarm and it was seven o'clock when we woke. Panic stations were in place as we quickly dressed and grabbed some toast and fruit from the dining room. Thank goodness one of the lads had a car and we scrambled in and headed for the climb starting point.

Arriving at seven forty five we raced from the overflowing car park and there was an officer standing at the start of the track who informed us that we were too late. He said, "You'll have to come back next year boys as the last group left an hour ago". Fortunately my two new mates were NZ SAS soldiers and told the officer that they were in peak assault condition and they could run all day if that was required of them, even up mountains. They said they could catch this walking group of ordinary people walking in under twenty minutes. As the first two hours was straight forward assent walking over regular ground the officer said, "OK, but what about your mate?" One of my new friends said, "no worries, he's as fit as we are and he's an Aussie physical education teacher and top rugby player". Their description of me was gilding the lily a bit as I had just completed the first of three years of my physical education course and I was a rugby player. I suppose I was a top player, as I was a 'legend in my own lunch box'!

Now back to 'Kili'.

Judy had lost energy with the food we had been eating for many months while travelling in Africa as she was low in vitamins Bs. She decided to join me for day one of the walk/climb of the mountain. The walk through the country side to higher farming land on day one to the first hut with me was all she thought she could manage.

Oh, how well prepared we were. Sailing jackets with hoods, jeans, suede casual shoes, thin gloves, tiny car torch, limited water, dehydrated food, rice, chocolate bars, camp gas and a pot, and a duffel bag for clothing . No guide. By the end of the first day I had a raging altitude headache. Judy was fine, no headache and feeling good. She decided that first night she wouldn't leave me, and shared my sleeping bag on the wooden slat bed (no mattress) in the hut and ate my chocolate.

We spent two more magical days as we started on some major steep climbing. The fabulous views by day and the cold penetrating into our bones at night recorded some vivid memories for me. We passed the tree line on the second day and the third day was often spent scrambling up loose ground.

The last thousand feet or so on Kilimanjaro has to be climbed at about two o'clock in the morning when the scree gravel has frozen, so you're not sliding about as much. Our small torch was our guiding light as we pushed hard ever upward. We felt we were getting closer to the summit and snow started to swirl around us with a wind. In a matter of about ten minutes the snow had became heavy and almost blinding.

Here we both were at nineteen thousand feet in a storm... in total darkness, with our only light source being a fading two dollar torch, dressed in jeans, regular cotton shirt, a jumper, sailing jacket with a hood, cotton socks, suede Hush Puppy style shoes and thin gloves. This was bizarre behaviour of crazy young adventurers who didn't see or even understand that what they were doing was dangerous.

Our feet and hands were freezing and Judy was afraid of frostbite on lots of her body parts. We had no goggles or even sunglasses and our eyes were not protected. We couldn't see as our puny torch had finally given out, so Judy called it quits and I had to see the sense in that too. We turned around and half guessed our way back as best we could, our steps now hard to find in the snow and darkness. After some time she turned around to her left and there was a vague impression of what appeared to be our hut, back up the slope a bit.

Free-wheeling works. There was a very suspicious fall away of land and snow just in front of us when Judy spotted what may have been our hut. We investigated later that morning in the light of day – so glad we stopped and made the detour to check out the hut possibility as in front of us was a nasty cliff sort of thing with a massive drop off.

Judy said after the event when we were safe in the third hut where we started the final assent from, that she just knew she had to have us stop and go back. In hindsight, this was a miracle.

So my wonderful wife in a matter of few weeks possibly saved my life three times. What a 'miracle worker' she was, my guardian angel.

Wow! When we let that mind of ours come into free-wheeling mode amazing results can emerge. I suggest you welcome them and foster them as our resources in this other ninety percent are brilliant. You can do this simply by sitting quietly and breathing deeply into your stomach while letting worries and stresses go out in your breath. To affirm 'I release, let go and move on' can help.

When you hand out an *Expect A Miracle* card to someone you can set up free-wheeling in the mind of that person because the thought on the card is so unexpected. You can sometimes see them actually move their bodies in some way as they process and reorganize their thoughts.

Nerve impulses fire forty million times per second in our subconscious mind and just forty per second in our conscious mind. The subconscious contains our imagination, our intuition and our possibility thinking so it behoves us, I think, to let the subconscious mind run free regularly. It can then give us ideas, impressions or pictures of where and how we can make the changes that we have decided on with our rational conscious mind. It also gives us new ways to move forward and these impulses are best listened to.

These are times when miracles happen.

Each day I write my miracles in my diary. If you have a diary or journal, write them down there because the more you write, the more good things will be attracted to you. Make up some positive affirmations for yourself about how you have your goals now, and repeat them at least once daily *with feeling* and set that subconscious mind in motion for your life to benefit. That works!

Write your goals down, perhaps each on the back of an *Expect A Miracle* card and read them often. I carry thirteen *Expect A Miracle* cards with a rubber band around them in my pocket constantly with the thirteen goals that are uppermost in my thoughts written on them. I read these goals often during the day.

Remember, set the goal, put the action steps in place and then celebrate the miracle. Woohoo! And then, give thanks. Whether it's thanks to another person, or thanks to your higher power, it is so powerful. Remember, a miracle is a wonder or a marvel, big or small, and it's simply an outpouring of positive energy.

Miracle Nine

Help enough others get their miracles and it's amazing what a positive life you create.

GOAL

GRATITUDE
Say
THANK YOU

TAKE
the
ACTION STEPS

CELEBRATE
the
"MIRACLE"

> *You need to be aware of what others are doing, applaud their efforts, acknowledge their successes, and encourage them in their pursuits. When we all help one another, everybody wins.*
>
> **Jim Stovall**

Number Nine

Help enough others get their miracles and it's amazing what a positive life you create.

It's fun helping people create miracles. It's a joy. And the amazing thing is that good things often come back to you in a way you least expect.

I love stories because they show the essence of what can happen, especially when you give the gift of an *Expect A Miracle* card.

A number of years ago I took a flight from Australia to the USA to speak at an exciting conference in New Jersey. I boarded the flight in Brisbane late morning on a Wednesday and had to make continual ongoing connections in Sydney, Auckland, Honolulu and Los Angeles before arriving at my destination, New York. I managed to stay awake during the hours between each leg of the flight, when I had to leave the aircraft, so I wouldn't sleep through the various connections. By the time I arrived in New York I had been travelling over thirty six hours.

The thing that always amazes me about travelling east from Australia to America is that you always arrive there on the same day, and earlier than the time you left Australia. Heading home is more confusing, as travelling west you actually lose a day of your life in the air. You can leave Los Angles at eleven o'clock Monday night, but you arrive in Sydney on Australia's east coast at six in the morning on Wednesday! Tuesday is a transit day you spend in the air that gets 'gobbled up' in time zone criss-crossing the globe.

Now, back to New York where I got off the last flight finally on a Wednesday afternoon at five o'clock at JFK airport. New York folks have a reputation for sometimes being abrupt, to the point, of even rude in the minds of some visitors to the city. It was full on rush hour and the human zoo was in full swing at that time of day at JFK. There were people moving everywhere, calling out, pushing, and rushing in all directions, largely oblivious to one another.

I went downstairs to the Ground Transportation Desk and it was about five deep with people. If you don't know how to go to your hotel, for example, you call in there and they tell you the best way to get to your destination. Three rotund African-American women were sitting on high stools behind the counter and people were loudly yelling things like "I want to go to Newark; I wanna go to Lake Success, and fast!"

Eventually, after about twenty minutes I eased my way up to the counter, put my hand in my pocket and pulled out one of my gift cards. "A gift for you Ma'am, Expect A Miracle." "Wow! Is this card for me brother?" she beamed. I said, "Yes Ma'am, this card is for you." And she said, "You must be born again brother?", "I'm definitely born Ma'am, I'm definitely born." "Oh, sisters! Look at this card!" as she was showing it to the other two women. "Do you have any more of these beautiful cards Sir?" I said, "Absolutely." Out came my beautiful little Expect A Miracle card holder and I gave each of the other two women their own cards.

"Girls, we gotta help this man! Now, where you goin' to Sir?" I said I needed to go to Teaneck, New Jersey and I understood it is probably an hour and a half from here. The first woman said, "Wow! You've got some choices Sir. The first choice is the bus. That's the cheapest, seventy-seven dollars. After the bus, you can take the shuttle and that's more expensive, then the taxi cab and that's more expensive, then the town car and that's more expensive, then the limo and that's more expensive, and finally the super stretch limo and that's more expensive. You can see they just keep goin on up in price."

I said, "Ok. I don't have to speak until tomorrow night, so there's no urgency and I'd love to see more of America because it's July, it's summer, it's five o'clock and it will be light till late so I can take time to see the sights. I'll take the bus please."

"Yeah, brother! Go for it girls! Let's hit the phones." Everyone else was totally ignored while my needs were being met. These three women were out there, working those phones unbelievably. Ten minutes went by and the large group of people waiting was really steaming about the attention these women were extolling on me.

The lead agent said, "Brother! Have I got a deal for you? I've got you a miracle." I said, "Thank you ma'am, what's the miracle?" She said, "You're going to Teaneck, New Jersey in a Super Limo!" I said, "Ma'am, I asked for the bus?" "Yes, Sir, but I got you the Super Limo for the same seventy-seven dollars!" This was not that long after the 9/11 incident when the Twin Towers went down and the limo services were taking a beating. This particular owner had four cars but there had been almost no call for any of his cars. He chose to keep one running, at cost, which he drove himself.

My directions were specific and I went to the curb side opposite the terminal building to wait for my Super Stretch Limo which was to arrive very shortly. On the curb side as I left the building, there they were, two dog-tired men who had been travelling in the same row three across beside me on each flight all the way across the Pacific Ocean and then across America, all the way from Brisbane. They had joined a long queue of about a hundred and fifty people to go to Manhattan by stop-start bus. Here I was, making my way through this very long queue to the other side of the road which was devoid of people as my *Super Stretch Shiny Silver Limo* slid into view.

The slick silver monster seated eighteen big people. It had two fully stocked bars, loads of snacks and two television sets. I eased into the back as the driver took my bags. The driver spoke to me from the front by microphone. He was great company. I moved up to the front end of the passenger seats and sat quite close to the sliding window. This gave my driver a direct communication channel with me instead of him having to use the microphone. He gave me a great tour all the way to New Jersey for an hour and a half. It was just brilliant.

As we drove on numerous freeways through residential areas of New York and New Jersey I thought of those three women who work each day on the Ground Transportation Desk at JFK in such a high stress environment. They had been so excited to receive their *Expect A Miracle* cards. It was amazing for me also to experience the positive joy that came out of this encounter with these three caring women. I continually observe beautiful responses from normal people who receive a special lift from receiving the simple gift of an *Expect A Miracle* card as they go about doing their job.

We finally arrived at the beautiful five star hotel where I was to speak the next evening. I thanked my driver and followed the Bell Man to the registration desk. The young man Robert who processed my registration was warm and friendly and asked me where I had flown from that day. When I told him I had been flying continuously for thirty six hours from the east coast of Australia and finally my drive from JFK in New York to the hotel, he struggled to imagine the distance, the time taken and the number of plane changes that were necessary.

As is my usual custom, I gave Robert my credit card and also a trusted gift of an Expect A Miracle card. I had a standard room booked with no special view. My stay was for five nights and I asked Robert, "what opportunity is there Robert for a complementary room upgrade?" His answer was, "just give me a minute Sir and I'll check with my Manager." Robert returned shortly after an exit to the back of house and asked me, "do you have another one of those special Expect A Miracle cards Sir for my manager". "Absolutely! I beamed."

Off went Robert again and this time on his return he had his Manager with him. The manager said to me, "Welcome Dr Hinwood, we have arranged the Presidential Suite for you for your five days with us, we trust that you will enjoy your stay with us." I thanked both Robert and his Manager for their generosity and was then taken by the Bell Man to my luxurious suite. It was a great stay.

I have heaps of fun New York stories. Here's another. This one happened a year before the last story. The group I was visiting and speaking for in New York and Florida had a limousine arranged for me and I was met at JFK Airport after another of my marathon Australia- USA flights.

This time we were heading out to Lake Success on Long Island. I asked the driver why the traffic was so heavy that night. "Yeah", he said "look, the New York Islanders (ice hockey team) are playing the New York Rangers tonight Sir." It was the local derby, Islanders from Long Island, Rangers from Manhattan. When these guys play, the game is sold out weeks before.

The traffic was heavy because of the game and also way more people than those who had tickets, have been out there attempting to buy tickets from the scalpers. They couldn't get tickets and they were on their way home. I said that I have to go to that game, and my hotel is across the road from the Coliseum where it will be played. My driver said "You won't get a ticket, believe me you can't get in". I said, "I have this little card here that says Expect A Miracle. I'll have a go".

On arriving at the hotel I left my bags with the concierge and crossed a huge parking lot to the Coliseum entrance. A whole series of ticket windows had slashes across them saying "SOLD OUT", "SOLD OUT", "SOLD OUT", "SOLD OUT".

There was one window in a corner that was up a tiny bit with no sold out sign on it. I walked over to this window and I bent down, put one hand on the sill and then pushed my other arm through the window where it could be seen inside the ticketing office. In this hand my fingers held the mighty Expect A Miracle card and I called out, "Hello, hello, anybody there? I've just arrived from Australia and I need a ticket to the game. Can you help me, please? Can you create a miracle for me?"

Not long after that the card disappeared from my fingers and the window was opened a little and a smiling face looked at me and said, "WOW ... that's a great little card. You want a ticket for the game man?" I said, "yeah, I've just came from Australia, surely there must be one spare ticket available?" "One minute Sir", and when she came back she said, "I got a choice for you of three; you can have behind the Rangers goal, behind the Islanders goal, or behind the Islander's bench four rows back". I said, "Thank you so much, I'll have the one behind the Islanders bench please". I bought the ticket and there was no price mark up; I just paid face value which was unbelievable. The woman loved her card and thanked me for adding hope to her life.

Next I went into the jammed packed arena where the noise was deafening and sat down. The man on my right said "What are you doing here? This is Bill's seat. Bill's not missed a game since the franchise was formed sixteen years ago". I said, "He has tonight buddy and I bought his ticket". Wow, I had a great night. The locals befriended the boy from Australia and looked after me like I was royalty.

The next day I was speaking to a group of chiropractors at a New York hotel about engagement, communication and relationships. I reminded them how important it is in life to ASK for what you want. Even when people say you can't have it or they can't do it or it's not possible, still ASK and you will be amazed at the outcomes. I also shared with them the power of the little white card with the three words on it, *Expect A Miracle.*

I shared with them the story of my experience the night before at the hockey game when the limo driver and the hotel concierge both told me that I was crazy in even trying to get a ticket to the game as everyone knows its been sold out for weeks. Even the scalpers had sold their tickets. There was still a chance as I had not personally asked for a ticket and the Expect A Miracle card is so powerful in creating something very special. I call the card a 'miracle magnet'!

My belief is that Expect A Miracle cards can take people to a different mental and emotional place when they are receptive. I believe it is a place of joy, of sharing and openness as well as friendship. This is the gift the card gives them unconditionally.

At the end of my presentation we went to lunch where a vibrant young woman told me how much she enjoyed my story about asking, even when the odds seem to be way against you. She asked me would I please have a spare *Expect A Miracle* card I could give her. You ask, you receive was my response. I gave her a card. She asked if I liked basketball. I said that I love it. She said, "Look, tonight the New York Knicks are playing the LA Lakers (the two top teams in the NBA at that time) and I have a spare ticket, if you want to come with me as my partner is in LA this week". My response was, "Great!" So she said, "Meet me at Madison Square Garden at 7pm tonight at the main entrance."

As we entered this famous sporting venue you could feel the excitement of the crowd, the music, the constant chatter of New Yorkers', the background noise, the smell of a sporting arena and the massive number of seats that were rapidly filling up.

The hustle and bustle of people moving up the entry alleys with their hot dogs, burgers, popcorn, beers and pop as they made their way to their seats was exciting in its own way. My host said to me as we were making our way to our seats, "I have a friend who is a movie producer and he lives half time here, half time in LA. If he is in LA tonight we can probably have his private box courtside". This was a very expensive piece of real estate back then, two seats and your own private butler who takes care for all your food and drink needs. My host had me wait at the end of the alley we entered as she spoke to the butler and then she waved me down. The box owner was in LA. This superlative box at court side that night was ours for this special game.

We were flicked with perspiration coming off the hair and bodies of the players when they came off onto their bench, we were so close. It was just a most magnificent game, very, very tight, another miracle gift to me who loves anything athletic. My new friend said she was delighted to return the favour of a miracle I had given her. I'm sure there is a giving and receiving cycle that happens in life continually.

When you put positivity out there, when you go for it, it's amazing what happens. I was helping these ladies at JFK by giving them a card that changed their day. The hotel check in agent and his manager were thrilled to receive their cards that changed their day. The hockey ticket seller loved her card; it was a surprise gift on a hectic night. I was helping the chiropractors understand how it's OK to ask. The outcome was they helped me too. We all can win.

My suggestion is that you get your own *Expect A Miracle* cards printed and start handing them out. I suggest that you write down three or more miracles every day in your diary or in your journal, and also read miracle stories. Read inspiring stories from the books at night or go to the website. Please write stories and post them on the website. This process I believe of telling your miracle stories by writing them down and sharing them with others opens up pathways and channels of expectancy in your brain that attracts more miracles into your life.

Set the goal, create the action steps, do them, and celebrate the miracles. "Wooohooo!!"

After your celebration, give thanks to those who supported you on your path.

If you complete the cycle it's brilliant what comes into your life.

That's the miracle!

Miracle 🔑 Ten

Abundance abounds ... there are plenty of miracles for us all.

GOAL

GRATITUDE
Say
THANK YOU

TAKE
the
ACTION STEPS

CELEBRATE
the
"MIRACLE"

> *It would probably amaze a lot of people if they know the inside story of a lot of 'rags to riches' entrepreneurs' lives as I do, to discover that just about the only reason for their meteoric success is simply getting into motion, before they were ready.*
>
> ### Dan Kennedy

Number Ten

Abundance abounds, there are plenty of miracles for us all.

My mother Ivy Hinwood was a short woman standing four feet ten and a half inches who was always full of life and loved to laugh a lot. In hindsight she was my great teacher and mentor of the *Expect A Miracle* concept. I remember when I was a child, my mother was always positive about what the future would be. When I was three, she decided to go back to work after having been a home mum for nine years. She took up the position of cook in the Pre-School I was starting at, which was a part of our local Congregational Church, close by to our home. She loved her work there and as a small boy I was so proud that my mum cooked all the beautiful food we ate.

She then moved from there and worked as a bookkeeper. That's what she had done all through her working life prior to having children.

When I was five and went to school, she bought her first shop. That shop was a delicatessen that had been bankrupted and had been shut for a number of months. She took over the lease on the shop with the stock, fixtures and fittings that remained of the 'dead' business coming as part of the lease. Within months, Ivy very quickly revitalized it into a thriving business. Over the next seven years she built it up into a rock solid 'cash cow' with loving service and entrepreneurial management. How did she do it and what did she do?

She was a miracle worker, who knew about abundance. She knew that abundance abounds and she knew there were plenty of miracles out there.

She was an entrepreneur who had wonderful practical ideas that were usually outside the traditional way of thinking of her day. She was so ahead of the pack.

Even as a three year old, I can still hear in my mind chatter from my father. This conservative sports journalist, would tell my mother, "These ideas you have Ivy will send us broke." My mum would always answer, "Don't worry Jack, I'll make us lots of money and it's all as safe as money in the bank". Ivy had savvy and always turned her left field ideas into profit making projects that were low or no cost items to get off the ground.

Through hard work and innovative thinking she went out and created miracles.

Now, here I am at five, its 1951 just after the end of World War Two in Sydney Australia and the only common take away food was fish and chips, only available from a fish shop. A few little milk bars made hamburgers; there were pies and sausage rolls from the bakery or cake shop or sandwiches from the delicatessen. That was the extent of take away food in Australia in 1951.

As her shop was next to our local train station which was a twenty minute ride to Sydney city, my Mum decided that she was going to make some take away food for people who worked in the city. They could pick meals up for dinner on their way home from work at night.

She did some market research of her customer base asking them, "How would you like to be able to pick up a hot rabbit on your way home from work at night?", Enthusiastically people replied, "Oh, I'd love a hot rabbit."

Back in those days very few people could afford to buy roasting chickens. Most people ate boiling chickens which were usually boiled in a big pot or cooked in a pressure cooker and afterwards placed in the oven for thirty minutes or so to be browned, like a roasted chicken. Chickens were expensive and not readily available in the shops except at Christmas and Easter which was usually by special order. Rabbits however were very, very cheap. When pressure cooked and then roasted and sliced and covered in gravy on your plate, it was hard to tell the difference between rabbit and chicken meat, especially if the rabbit had been braised, boiled or pressure cooked in a mixture of milk and water.

In the late 1940s and 1950s wild rabbits were in plague proportions in many parts of Australia. They were a great source of very clean, lean and tasty meat. They were totally organic by today's standards. I remember my mum sold rabbits in pieces as well as whole rabbits.

Rabbits in those days were only sold by the meat distributors in pairs to the retailers and they were delivered in big long trays. I always loved opening the fridge after the man from the Riverstone Meat Company had delivered the rabbits so I could count them.

My mum started her day early in the morning and rabbit cooking was always first up on her list. Each run with the large pressure cooker saw three rabbits prepared, each one coiled into a circle shape to fit into the cooker. She cooked the rabbits, took them out and stockpiled them to put into the oven in the late afternoon to brown them ready for collection. Customers would be coming from work and take them home. They would queue up to collect their hot rabbit orders every week day evening between 4.30pm and 6pm.

By the way there were no plastic bags in those days. The hot rabbits were first wrapped in greaseproof paper and then gleaming white shiny wrapping paper the same as was the meat from the butcher and the fish and chips from the fish shop.

Ivy Hinwood in Edwin Street, Croydon was the Colonel Sanders of the early 1950's in Australia.

She also created Subway style giant rolls. There were thousands of refugees who fled to Australia after World War Two. These people didn't start arriving till nineteen forty seven. In nineteen fifty one the refugees who arrived were mainly from the United Kingdom and Europe. Those from Europe who didn't speak English were referred to as 'reffo's'.

One particular day a man visited Ivy's shop and introduced himself s a baker who had recently arrived in Australia to create a new home after the ravages of the war in his home country of Czechoslovakia. Mr Pitsika had just opened *Red Rose Bakery* in a suburb not far away and he was visiting delicatessens in his surrounding area to see if they would be interested in stocking continental style bread, which was all very new in Australia at that time.

People purchased their bread in those days off the local horse drawn cart that the local baker delivered from door to door in each city suburb. Most suburbs had their own bakery and it was the days before supermarkets. You could also buy bread from local milk bars and delicatessens.

 As Ivy was a visionary and always looking at how she could increase her trade by having a USP (*Unique Selling Position*) that was different to her opposition she immediately saw the Vienna bread in its various varieties as an excellent opportunity. The other two delicatessens were not interested as everyone only wanted white or brown bread in square or high top varieties.

Mr Pitsika also shared with Ivy that he made half-size Vienna loaves, a bit shorter and half the girth of a normal Vienna loaf and a bit pointy at the ends. They looked just like a pregnant Subway foot long roll. Instead of two regular rolls for lunch, Ivy saw these large and unique Vienna rolls as a wonderful option and great talking point. She said, "Yes, let's do it."She became one of the biggest customers of Red Rose Bakery within a few months.

My Mum, the 'miracle woman' created yet another outstanding yummy delight that the big meat eaters of the day adored. In the nineteen fifties most families ate meat at least twice a day and many families like our family, ate meat three times a day. Ivy's delights were rissoles, real whoppers... full of sausage meat, mixed herbs and lots of chopped onion. They had no breadcrumbs as fillers and they were big, fat, juicy and scrumptious!

My Mum did all this cooking on a regular four burner gas stove with an oven. My dad cut the side out of a four gallon kerosene tin with the lid screwed on at the end and sealed. It was filled up with dripping and the rissoles were dropped in like fish and chips in a deep fryer.

The new half Vienna loaves were perfect with two rissoles each cut in half, adding tomato sauce, mustard and salad for some and a great meal was ready to down the hatch. Truck drivers, tradesmen, commercial travelers and many more would queue up at lunch time for the 'big roll'. The word of mouth referral grew very quickly and people travelled miles for the delights.

Here was a creative woman with an amazing clientele. She knew how to create abundance and she always expected miracles, and received them.

I was the last to leave home at twenty when I was transferred from Sydney to teach in the outback at Broken Hill. My folks then sold up in Sydney and moved to our family holiday house on the beach a couple of hours north of Sydney. Ivy was bored as my dad commuted to work in Sydney each day and she felt there was only so much bridge and lawn bowls she could play each week.

She purchased a run-down card shop in their local shopping centre that she saw loads of upside potential in. In the mid nineteen sixties newsagents were the place you went to if you wanted to buy a lottery ticket. She applied to the State Lottery's Office and got a license, to sell lottery tickets in the card shop.

Their town had a big licensed bowling club and my father was the President and my mum a team selector in the women's section of the club. They were both very well known in a community with a high number of retirees.

The largest demographic group in Australia, who gambles, is retiree's and they love buying lottery tickets. People of that generation love cards with sayings and great words in them. People would come into Ivy's shop and she would always ask what the card was for. She knew her card stock back to front. She would lead her customer to a particular card and then say, "I believe this is good for you, I'll read the verse to you." The people who would line up had no trouble saying "Yes".

They just knew that Ivy would always do the best by them and make a great choice on their behalf.

Once again she quickly created a thriving business attracting people with loving service and care. She could create miracles is helping people with often difficult card choices. She was a beautiful woman, who just had this skill of loving and caring for people. She was a miracle worker with take-away food that was nutritious and wholesome and on the cutting edge of a new way of life as people started to get busier and television was entering our lives.

She taught me a huge amount about having a positive mental attitude and always displaying gratitude. She always spent time thanking people. She sent thank you cards back then. Did many people send thank you cards? My mother did. She loved to make people feel good about themselves. She said, "Johnny, if you thank people for what they do for you, it's amazing how much more they want to do for you."

If my mum had seen the *Expect A Miracle* card, I know that she would have loved it and she would have handed them out in a never ending manner .She would have been selling them in packs. She would have become a 'Miracle Emissary'

If you don't have any Expect A Miracle cards, go to our website and get some for free or use the template provided. Give it to your printer and start handing them out. Write down three or more miracles that happen to you each day, no matter how tiny they are. Write down some goals on the back of *Expect A Miracle* cards. Create a pictorial picture, a life map or a treasure map, a collage of pictures and words of how you want your life to look like in the next five years. Read your goals every day. Read a miracle story before you go to bed each night to fertilize your mind as you sleep. Remember to set the goal, take the action steps, and celebrate "Wohooooo!"Acknowledge the outcome you receive, the miracle you get. Give thanks.

Attitude and Gratitude will help you to move forward. Power on!

Miracle 🗝 Eleven

When you are totally open to receiving miracles, it's astounding how they find their way to you and you become a 'miracle magnet'.

GOAL

GRATITUDE
Say
THANK YOU

TAKE
the
ACTION STEPS

CELEBRATE
the
"MIRACLE"

When we set out to do the best we can do, it is inevitable that great opportunity finds us because we are doing what truly makes us happy. We're in alignment and ready for the opportunities that life puts in our path.

Josh Hinds

Number Eleven

When you are totally open to receiving miracles it is astounding how they find you and come to you and you become a miracle magnet.

They just do! Your antenna goes up and you say, "I'm here, I'm here... ready to receive miracles, just send them to me." And they do! Things just happen because you are ready to receive. Of course we have to take actions towards them as well – we aren't saying to do nothing to help yourself.

We've talked about having no 'hang-ups' about mistakes, rather having 'learning experiences'. If you are concerned you might fail, and what people might think, or you might be wondering how you can ever get back on top again after failing, you may only play life safely and not take the smallest chance.

What role do expectations and expectancy play in this key?

Expectation is a belief that is centred on the future and it may or may not be realistic. A less advantageous result can give rise to disappointment. If something happens that is not at all expected it is a surprise.

Expectancy is the faith that better efforts will result in better performance and outcomes. Expectancy is influenced by factors such as possession of appropriate skills for performing the job, availability of the right resources, availability of all necessary information and getting the required support for completing the job.

Victor Vroom of the Yale School of Management postulated the Expectancy Theory (1964) explaining that there are mental processes regarding choice, or choosing. It explains the processes that an individual undergoes to make choices. Expectancy theory proposes that a person will decide to behave or act in a certain way because they are motivated to select a specific behaviour over other behaviours. This is due to what they expect the result of that selected behaviour will be. In essence, the motivation of the behaviour selection is determined by the desirability of the outcome. At the core of the theory is the cognitive process of how an individual processes the different motivational elements.

The great platform speaker Earl Nightingale said, "The timid feeders live in the tranquil, easy, non-challenging lagoon and the strong fish live outside the lagoon, where the waves pound the coral reef. They are the ones who have to fight the current and do whatever else is necessary if they hope to become large, strong, stay alive and flourish. The lagoon dwellers don't become the big, strong fish of the wide challenging ocean."

There is a beautiful story of a South Australian professional fisherman who was out in the Great Australian Bight and he found a four metre Great White shark badly entangled in fishing nets. He valued and loved sharks so he didn't hesitate to lean way out and cut away the netting, freeing the huge creature.

The freed shark leaped out of the water, breaching like a whale in its joy, looking him in the eye – a magical moment indeed.

Afterwards, whenever the fisherman appeared in his boat out at sea, the shark came to greet him. He developed a passionate relationship with this monster of the sea and the shark would come alongside his boat and put its head out of the water seeking a rub from its friend. His friend obliged and the relationship prospered.

 This gentleman's passion when he wasn't out fishing was kayaking out at sea in his three point eight metre kayak. He would be out there, communing with the elements, and who would appear? His mascot, his friend, the Great White shark, and wherever he went his friend was there, cruising on the surface, following him and circling.

There are photos of this, and of the man reaching out of his boat to tickle the shark! A French magazine had heard about the interactions and travelled to Australia to experience the interaction first hand alongside the fisherman and write an article on him and record the remarkable moments. Here was this massive Great White coming to his boat, offering his snout to have it patted!

The fisherman said his only problem now is that his haul of fish now wasn't as good as in the past as his new found his friend was scaring some schools of fish away.

This shark knew when the man was at sea. This is similar to the herd of thirty one elephants in South Africa in late 2012, lead by a matriarch who knew when their friend Lawrence Anthony, 'The Elephant Whisperer', had died. The elephants walked over twelve miles through the bush on the reserve where they lived to stand in a paddock beside his family home. They stayed for two days, without food and water, outside his house, paying their respects it would seem.

The way these communications happen isn't a mystery anymore, thanks to quantum physics. Our thoughts of openness to receiving miracles work just like the animals' receiving men's thoughts. You might think of yourself like an antenna, giving out and receiving messages, and the more open your thoughts are to giving and receiving good things, the more it will happen. You are a force of nature like everyone else.

Miracle 🗝 Twelve

Miracles come when you least expect them ... make them welcome whenever they arrive.

GOAL

GRATITUDE
Say
THANK YOU

TAKE
the
ACTION STEPS

CELEBRATE
the
"MIRACLE"

Gratitude can lead to feelings of love, appreciation, generosity, and compassion, which further reopen our hearts and help rewire our brains to fire in more positive ways.

Melanie Greenberg

Number Twelve

Miracles come when you least expect them. Make them welcome whenever they arrive.

This key is centred on you gaining a better understanding of the concept of expectation, 'I want this'. If your expectation is too strong and you are saying 'I want this and nothing else', sometimes you will get the nothing else. If you live in a time and place of expectancy – not expectation - it is amazing the miracles that will show up in your space. Just seeing what shows up after you have asked, is a key. Something will show up, however accepting the miracles in whatever form it takes, is expectancy.

Big, small or intermediate, make the miracles welcome! Then more and more good things will find their way to you. It just happens that way! When you are open to receiving, things can come into your space.

There is a statement I use that says, 'it is wonderful to be crazy, but not stupid'.

I'm going to tell you a story which I often think about. I was an eighteen year old physical education student, a long time ago. I had left a rugby game I had played in on a wintry Saturday afternoon. It was just starting to get dark. I was going to a party in my old 1952 Morris Oxford car and bam, a flat tire happened. I pulled over, jacked the car up and proceeded to take the wheel off. I carefully took off the five wheel nuts and put them into the hubcap. My Dad had taught me to turn the hubcap over and put the wheel nuts into the dish for safekeeping until they were needed. Then you put the replacement wheel back onto the car. That was a fine idea until I had to give the flat tire an extra bit of a tug as it was stuck.

The wheel came off at an angle and with some speed once it became unstuck. The result was that the wheel knocked the upturned hubcap. I happened to be parked next to a wide drainage grate and the nuts spilled out of the hubcap and rattled through the grate, into the void underneath, plop, plop, plop, plop, plop. It was bad happening after five o'clock on a Saturday evening. In those days everything was shut up and wouldn't open again until Monday morning. I lost the lot, never to be recovered. I wasn't a happy camper. All I could do was lock the car and leave it jacked up in the street until Monday.

The next thought was, how do I get to the party? In the early nineteen sixties, hitching a ride was common place and people always picked you up in no time at all.

I couldn't figure out why no one was picking me up. After about twenty minutes and no success in getting a lift, I heard a voice coming from behind a three metre high wire fence behind me. The person was laughing and then said, "Mate, no one will pick you up here, this is the crazy farm. They think you are one of us loony's. Look at the sign above your head mate". Sure enough, I looked up and saw the sign, Callum Park Mental Asylum. The voice materialised into a shortish man, and he said, "Mate, you can still drive your car". My internal dialogue wondered very strongly, what would this man know? That little voice in my head that talks to me from time to time, that voice that can be very judgemental at times went into high gear. I was thinking, 'what would this idiot, this guy know about this'.

He continued, "Mate, you can go around the other three wheels, take one nut off each from those wheels and they will have four nuts each, and put the three nuts you now have on your spare wheel in a triangle to fix it onto the car. You could drive to Melbourne with three nuts on that wheel. Do them up tight, she'll be right. And where are you going mate?" he said. "I'm going to a party with lots of chicks." "Go for it mate, have a good weekend. Then Monday buy some nuts and she'll be sweet".

I said, "You're a miracle man". He said, "Mate, we all know we're in here because we're crazy, but mate, most of us aren't stupid."

Here I was at aged eighteen, and I learnt that there isn't anything wrong with stretching boundaries in my life in ways that others might think crazy, but that doesn't mean this is stupid behaviour. I've translated this to mean that we can live on the edge and do some different things, but assess the risks before starting so they are not silly or foolhardy risks.

In 2012 in the time leading up to the London Olympics, I watched an insightful interview with the Australian Olympic Sailing Coach. Sailing was the sport with the least money spent on it, yet these skilled sailors won the most gold medals for Australia. It was an amazing sailing result. People were asking how this had come about. Not surprisingly we had a brilliant sailing coach, a Ukrainian, Victor Kovalenko. He had helped Ukraine to more sailing medals than anyone else had won, in his time as coach there. He is just one amazing coach. He came to Australia in 1997 to coach our four hundred and seventy Class men's and women's crews. After these crews both won Gold medals at the Sydney 2000 Olympics and world championships he was named National Head Coach. He was warmly welcomed by our sailing fraternity for his transformational approach to coaching.

In the lead up to the London Olympics I saw a television interview with the sixty year old where he was asked, "how do you have this incredible success, how can you be so far ahead of everyone else with your results in coaching?" His reply was that it is because of his attitude. He is seen out early on the harbour every training day in his small craft, yelling instructions into his megaphone. He is totally in love with what he is doing. It is not work for him, it is joy.

He was asked, "There has to be some ingredient, some special magic you have, can you share that?" He said, "Yes, I will share the secret. The key is that it's OK to be crazy, but I also know that I'm not stupid."

He went on to explain that you have to live on the edge and perform on the edge if you want to be number one in the world in your sport or you want to be the Olympic champion and go home with the gold medal. You need to do some things that most others would believe are crazy.

I was stunned when I heard him say this as he had used the same principle to great success that I had learned from an inmate of a mental institution almost fifty years ago. He said, and I paraphrase, that he was happy to go to the edge himself, to push his charges to the edge, to do things out of the box that other sailing coaches would not do, all to lead his charges to great things in sailing, and further, to use these skills to create successful lives outside of sailing.

Laughter is a great healer. There is a great deal of research to show that when we laugh we produce endorphins. These are hormones naturally made in our bodies and they are up to three thousand times more powerful than opiates. I know as a chiropractor that endorphins are produced by the body to handle pain. Laughing changes the space the patient is in, mentally and emotionally. Laughter is a miracle provider in many ways.

In our chiropractic practice over the years we have used laughter therapy to help people who are emotionally drained and not in a 'good personal space' to help them change their state of well-being.

In the early 1980s we attended a workshop with Dr Dale Anderson who had practiced as an orthopaedic surgeon in the USA for many years. He realised he could achieve great results with laughter for pain relief, instead of using drugs or surgery often. He had his patients laugh for fifteen seconds, really laugh, gut wrenching laughter with their torso bending forward, thigh slapping laughter, three times a day for quite a period of time. The patients were to start with their hands over their heads, preferably in front of a mirror, they were to think of something really funny and go for it. They could use a funny video to get started if they needed to. He found their pain levels usually came under control, and often, quite rapidly.

Dr Anderson was on a lecture tour sponsored by the Australian Wellness Foundation who were interested in how people could get well and stay well, naturally.

When patients who came to our chiropractic practice we would give them an Expect A Miracle card and tell them the three rules of our office. Rule1: Smile... Expect A Miracle; Rule 2: Smile at every opportunity... Expect A Miracle; Rule 3: Refer to Rules 1 and 2.

For people having trouble following the rules, a laughter therapy session was the happy consequence. They were instructed to think of something funny, and if they couldn't do that, I would say, "well, you will soon laugh because what I'm about to do with you will make you guffaw at me". I would demonstrate and then have them join in. We did *real* laughter, often laughing till tears rolled down our cheeks. Invariably people in other parts of the clinic had a laugh with us as the sounds are so infectious. How healing for a practice!

Grumpy people were often given the same treat, sometimes laughing at us till they found their own sense of the ridiculous to laugh with. It's truly amazing what happens, how the grumpiness transforms into smiles, standing taller and having great memories. Miracles of healing, large and small abound.

Norman Cousins was a theatre critic in New York .In the 1960s he developed cancer. A few of his friends had gone the medical route with their cancers but he chose not to do so. Norman had heard about endorphins and laughter therapy, so he stayed in an apartment and had friends bring him endless videos that made him laugh; The Three Stooges and other funny people of his day and recent past. All his waking hours, laughter was the goal and the healer. He laughed, and laughed and laughed and laughed himself well. A couple of months later he was in remission and stayed well. He knew his body could produce the chemicals it needed to beat the cancer.

Laughter is a useful tool that can be used by people wanting a mood change to support them to move from their current state of not feeling the best they could be to a healthier state where they feel alive. We don't have to be unwell to benefit from laughter. We can use laughter as one of the tools to keep ourselves well and more energetic. It produces miracles.

Miracle 🔑 Thirteen

Start telling people you come into contact with to Expect A Miracle. This will work like a boomerang and come back to you as you continue to spread the miracle expectancy.

GOAL

TAKE
the
ACTION STEPS

GRATITUDE
Say
THANK YOU

CELEBRATE
the
"MIRACLE"

Every memorable act in the world is a triumph of enthusiasm. Nothing great was ever achieved without it because it gives any challenge or any occupation, no matter how frightening or difficult, a new meaning. Without enthusiasm you are doomed to a life of mediocrity but with it you can accomplish miracles.

Og Mandino

Number Thirteen

Start telling people you come into contact with to Expect A Miracle. This will work like a boomerang and come back to you as you continue to spread the miracle expectancy.

The more we spread the word, the more we engage people to consciously think about miracles that they would like to experience in their lives, the more miracles they create for themselves by focusing their mindset on the things that they truly want.

Not long ago, Judy and I went to Phuket, Thailand, to speak at the Wellness Festival and at the Atmanjai Wellness Centre.

At the International Airport in Brisbane our check in luggage was hopelessly overweight with books and other materials we needed for our speaking engagement. The check-in agent was doing everything she could to accommodate the problem but we were going to have to pay a lot for excess baggage. My hand luggage was seventeen kilos, we were allowed seven, and Judy's was also way over the limit. There was a blitz happening downstairs at Customs and Immigration the agent informed us. They were weighing all the hand luggage.

Along came the Check In supervisor who was a very stately woman, mid to late sixties, grey hair, elegant, and looked the part. Not officious, just extremely efficient. She asked if there was a problem. "No", I said, "your agent is doing a great job. We're on our way to Thailand to speak at a conference and our baggage is a little overweight". Thank goodness she didn't ask me to define the word 'little'. I gave her an Expect A

Miracle card too, just as I had given the check in agent even before I placed our bags on the luggage belt.

The Supervisor said. "I know you!" She put her hand into a pocket and took out a very will worn Expect A Miracle card, saying "you probably don't remember, but you gave me this quite a number of years ago here at the airport and I've always carried it with me. It's been a great help. All I can do is say thank you; it's been a lifesaver many times." To our Check In Agent she said, "whatever is there, just check it through". Whoo, hoo, thank you precious card. A lovely little miracle, and off we went to do our speaking in Phuket with all our seminar materials and books intact.

A number of years ago when Australia's second biggest domestic carrier Ansett was flying the skies I gave an Expect A Miracle card to an Ansett Supervisor when I was once again struggling with an overweight problem. He was so excited on receiving the card he asked me if I could supply him with enough cards to place them on the wall behind each Check In Agent. I happily obliged, and for the next two years until the check in area was totally remodeled, the Expect A Miracle cards held pride of place at Ansett, Brisbane Airport.

In my second last day of clinical practice, before I went into full time coaching and mentoring with chiropractors, I saw a new client. I'm going to call her Annette and she was sent by a friend of ours, Yvonne who was a much respected psychic. Yvonne really knew the power of chiropractic and she sent us people who had 'been everywhere and done everything' for their problem. Some of these problems were very different from the usual cases we saw.

In came this twenty nine year old beautiful woman and she had been everywhere attempting to get help with her problem. I wondered what I was going to do with her. The problem? Annette had had sex four times in her life and each time it was "like ramming a red hot poker into my vagina" she told me. The pain was excruciating. She just couldn't have sex, though she wanted a relationship and children. She thought perhaps she needed to adopt children but she wanted a relationship with a male partner where healthy sex was part of their loving relationship.

I did my usual chiropractic examination, took x-rays, ran a thermal scan and then did something supplemental that I do with cases that are out of the usual mold. It is N.E.T., Neuro Emotional Technique. Throughout life we can get blockages in our nervous system from the spill- over effect of physical, mental, emotional or spiritual events that rock us in some way. They can be major events or tiny events. For example, at three years old my great playmates' father was given an immediate transfer in his work, across the country. The trouble was, my family was away on holidays. We came back and the family was gone. I was heartbroken, especially as my friend didn't say goodbye. Sure, I got over it, but that emotion was locked in my body and released later by N.E.T.

Body organs are known to carry emotions, for example, the liver can carry anger and the gall bladder, resentment. I did some N.E.T. on this young woman. I asked her questions and muscle tested her bodies responses. The arm I was muscle testing to monitor her responses was either going weak or staying strong. If there is a problem, the arm goes weak, if not, it stays strong. I know, this sounds like voodoo to some people, but we simply tap into the natural energies of the body. It's like we have a torch with three batteries; one battery dies and the torch doesn't work, despite two good batteries. The energy flow is interrupted.

By muscle testing I found which organ and which emotion was involved, her age when the event happened, the family member involved with her and what happened. This is all recorded in the subconscious so the body responds very rapidly. The woman had been raped at six years old by her uncle who was babysitting her. She had never told anybody about the event. She had just blocked it off and had carried her emotional scars of the molestation since then. Whenever she had attempted to have sex the scar reared up. She was six years old again, wounded, in pain, unworthy, unclean, betrayed. Once the specific problem had been identified very specific and simple chiropractic work released the negative energy from her gallbladder. The person didn't feel a thing. I followed by asking the same questions as before and her arm remained strong throughout. All released and completed. I tested for more negative emotions, none were involved.

I told her I believed she was free now to enjoy sexual relations and lead a normal life. I sent her home with an Expect A Miracle card.

Normally after a first adjustment I call my patients in the early evening of the same day to see if there are any questions. Annette had none and said she was amazed at how I had found the problem and that she felt like a different person now, a huge weight had been lifted off her. At nine thirty that night I received a phone call from Annette who laughed and said "I just had to call you. I'm in the middle of having sex and it is fantastic. It is amazing. Thank you, thank you." I said "Annette, correct me if I'm wrong but you've put some poor bloke on hold so you could phone me and tell me how great sex is?" "Yeah, yeah" she said. I said, "hang up right now, and let this poor bloke get on with things, and thanks for calling!" The next day I saw her again then handed her case to the incoming chiropractors.

Several years later I was playing Santa at a Christmas party at our friend Yvonne's house and I was handing out gifts to the children as they sat on my knee. After about half an hour two little boys were left, such gorgeous boys, and I gave them their gifts. After I had changed from my Santa outfit and came back into the party, I was tapped on my shoulder. I turned to hear, "John, you don't remember me, do you?" It twigged, Annette of the memorable phone call, and she was radiantly smiling. She was with a man, and I don't know why I did this, but I said, "and you are the bloke she put on hold to phone the chiropractor. I bet you thought that was the kinkiest thing that had ever happened to you". "Oh, yes", he said. Annette took my hands in hers and said "what I need to tell you is this", as she started to cry. "Those two little boys who were the last ones on your lap and you gave gifts to are our sons. Without what you did for me that day, we wouldn't have a family" and the three of us cried together. Chiropractic is surely marvelous and this was her miracle.

We never know how we help some people. You will be involved with helping people and you will create ripple results – some you will know about, some you won't.

I ask you to take time now to write a miracle story of something that has happened to you. Please write it now or at latest within twenty four hours. Put a small amount of time aside, write – we have all had miracles happen to us - then email the story to us or put it on our website. Yes, there are prizes for weekly, monthly and annual "Readers' Choice" stories. On the website you can join the Miracle Mindset Private Members Club with lots of benefits. Please share your miracles with the world to bring more in.

People say that things change in their lives since reading about others miracles. The more we think about miracles, the more they boomerang back to us, as well. Expressing a miracle in writing is very powerful.

Arthur Ashe, the great tennis player, said that we have to get to the stage in life that winning the match is not as important as playing the match, as participating.

Share Your Miracle Stories

Share your miracle stories with the rest of the world. If you have a miracle story of your own, or someone else's, that you feel would enhance the lives of others, please post it on www.expectamiracle.com.

The best stories each year will be in future volumes of **You Can Expect A Miracle**.

An added benefit of submitting your stories to the website is that you could **win prizes** if you are chosen as the winner of the **Readers' Choice Story of the Week, Month and Year**.

The most read story each week from all those that have previously not won a prize will be awarded the **Readers' Choice Story of the Week** and will be featured on www.expectamiracle.com.

Our Judging Panel will select the best story of the weekly winners of the previous month and the author will be awarded **Readers' Choice Story of the Month**.

Each December our readers from around the world select the **Story of the Year by casting their votes** for the best of the 12 Story of the Month winners.

WINNERS PRIZES ... WEEKLY, MONTHLY, YEARLY

The **52** Weekly Winners receive the e-book edition of **You Can EXPECT A MIRACLE** ... The Book to Change Your Life.

The Monthly Winners **receive** the e-book editions of the next 6 **You Can EXPECT A MIRACLE** books ... Unexpected Miracles, Yes YOU Can, Insights Into Life, 201 Miracle Messages from A to Z, 13 Keys to Becoming a Miracle Magnet, With Chiropractic.

The Yearly Winner will receive the **Story of the Year "Miracle Award"** special trophy as #1 ranking miracle story of the year.

Visit our Website

www.expectamiracle.com

If you know someone who has a heartfelt or dynamite story to tell, please pass the website address on to them and invite them to join us in energizing the mental, emotional and spiritual health of people around the world.

I would appreciate you emailing your address book about this amazing site, and please ask your friends and colleagues to spread the positivity.

Thanks in advance.

If you register on the website, you will receive our **Expect a Miracle Monthly Newsletter** ... **"The Miracle Messenger"**.

The Prestigious Story of the Year "Miracle Award"

Each December, our readers from around the world select the **Story of the Year by casting their votes** for the best of the 12 Story of the Month winners.

The **Yearly Winner** will receive the **Story of the Year "Miracle Award" special trophy** as #1 ranking miracle story of the year, and will be featured on the website and in 'The Miracle Messenger' newsletter.

Simply submit your miracle story into the appropriate category on the website or email your story to: admin@expectamriacle.com

Each week our readers choose a story of the week,

"Readers' Choice Story of the Week".

Not only are there hundreds of **written stories** you can browse and enjoy, there are also endless numbers of **video stories** you can watch and feel the raw emotion of individuals sharing their miracles.

Looking for a Speaker for Your Next Conference, Seminar or Workshop?

You can contact Dr John Hinwood at
john@expectamiracle.com

for speaking engagements.

Dr Scott Walker, the Founder of Neuro Emotional Technique from California, USA wrote this note after I spoke to his seminar group about *Expecting Miracles* in November 2007.

"I was attending a *NET SUCCESS* Chiropractic Seminar in Northern New South Wales, Australia. Dr John Hinwood was presenting to the group and asked if there were any volunteers from this group of over 100 chiropractors who would be willing to share a miracle they had witnessed in their lives.

As is typical in such a group, a few brave souls who were not afraid of speaking in public got up and shared some miracles they had seen. Fair enough so far. Most of the attendees said nothing, but applauded the doctors who did share. Then Dr Hinwood asked the audience if they would write down any miracles they had witnessed on a piece of paper.

I was overwhelmed. Why? Without an iota of hesitancy, every single one of the hundred attendees immediately put pen to paper to write about a miracle they had witnessed. There was no pondering or scratching of heads wondering how to phrase things, but an instant and ongoing flow of written descriptions. Apparently, miracles were not hard to come by!

Imagine over one hundred people being able to recall a miracle they had witnessed at the drop of a hat. It appeared that each of them could have come up with several miracles.

That so many people were Instantly able to recount one miracle was and is miraculous in its own right."

Dr John Hinwood

Expect A Miracle

PO Box 4125

Forest Lake Qld 4078

Australia

Phone:+ 61 3879 0069

Fax: +61 7 3714 9700

Email: admin@expectamiracle.com

Website: www.expectamiracle.com

To Order Additional Copies of this Book

If you would like to order additional copies of this book, either single copies or volume quantities for gift giving, please email us at info@expectamiracle.com or visit us at www.expectamiracle.com.

About the Authors

Drs Judy and John Hinwood are authors, international speakers, mentors, coaches and consultants whose clients are largely health-care professionals. Drs Hinwood started their careers in the 1960s as teachers in Australia, England, South Africa and Canada before commencing their Chiropractic studies in Canada in the mid- 1970s.

They travelled extensively all over the world off the beaten track from 1969 to 1973 setting out overland from Australia through Asia and onto Europe and spent time in Eastern Europe and Russia during the Cold War. They drove their Land Rover trans-Africa from London to South Africa and then spent many months travelling by public transport all over South America and the Caribbean before arriving in Toronto, Canada in the fall of 1973.

In late 1978 John and Judy returned to Australia and set up chiropractic practices in rural and then, metropolitan communities.

In 1985, they travelled to Chile and found three older children, Shavela, Ignacio and Rodrigo in orphanages whom they then adopted to have an instant family.

Judy and John Hinwood are the Founders of The Centre for Powerful Practices which they established in 1991. They have an extensive client base worldwide. They have published seven books and multi-media packages on practice management.

Judy is the Founder of Mind Your Life which gives tools and strategies for focussed well-being and positivity training. www.mind-yourlife.com.au.

John is the Founder of Expect A Miracle School and the exciting website he launched in November 2007 www.expectamiracle.com that is a huge storehouse of amazing stories of miracles that have happened in people's lives. The stories are spreading positivity to people around the world. His book You Can Expect A Miracle ...The Book to Change Your Life, was released in 2008 and is an international best-seller.

They have received many awards from chiropractic organisations around the world and are the recipients of the Humanitarian Award in Australia and the US for their services to the chiropractic profession worldwide.

As international speakers they inspire their audiences into taking practical action steps to move their lives to new levels. Their perspectives, humour, observations, insights into life and entertaining stories are from the heart and they inspire and motivate people into taking positive action steps.

Print Your Own Expect a Miracle Cards

I started this mission of handing out these cards over twenty five years ago, and they have changed my life and the lives of thousands of people with the very simple, yet extremely powerful use of three amazing words. Hope is something we all need continually throughout our lives.

The amazing positive stories and outcomes as a result of people receiving these cards and then creating a miracle through their awareness and shift in consciousness needs to be shared with the broader community. As messengers of hope in the community, we enhance people's lives by supporting all those we come in contact with to experience enhanced physical, mental, emotional and spiritual wellbeing.

Using these little cards as gifts can change YOUR life and the lives of many people you come in contact with during your daily interactions in life.

The power in the card is that it does not have your name on it. It's not about you. It's about the receiver Expecting A Miracle! If you want to spread this message of hope and positivity, then print your own cards so that you can start handing them out.

Many people have asked me over the years if they could copy the idea, and I've said, "Absolutely, please do!"

The card looks like this, and it is blank on the other side.

Expect A Miracle

An easy way to print your own cards is to go to our companion website www.expectamiracle.com

Go to the link in the footer on the homepage that says Expect A Miracle Cards and email the template to yourself so you can print off your own cards on your home or office printer or email the template to your printer and start handing cards out.

All you need to do is print them from the PDF page that is set out ready for you to use. Print the cards on 350 gsm (or thicker) card stock coated on one side and matt on the blank side. The font used on these cards is my personally designed font, so use the PDF available on the website to print your cards from. The best colour is reflex blue.

Your other choice is to email the PDF file to your printer and supply the printer with the following information: the Expect A Miracle cards are printed on 350 gsm Cast Coat stock or similar (gloss on one side and matt on the other). The blue is Pantone 281c, which is printed digitally with breakdown c100, m72, y0, k32.

Make sure you leave the back of the card blank. Having only the three words "Expect A Miracle" on the card gives it awesome power.

Never doubt that a small group of thoughtful people could change the world.

Indeed, it's the only thing that ever has.

Margaret Mead

Create Miracles For Others ...

Give the Gift of
You Can ... EXPECT A MIRACLE

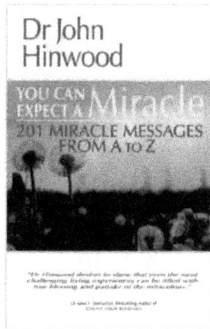

Available on www.amazon.com or www.expectamiracle.com

Pure Inspiration ...

Share the Gift of a Book

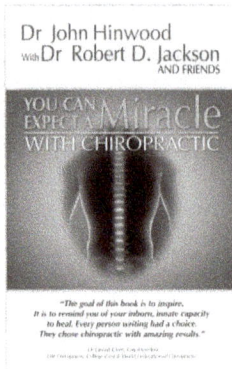

Dr John Hinwood
With Dr Robert D. Jackson
AND FRIENDS

YOU CAN EXPECT A Miracle
WITH CHIROPRACTIC

"The goal of this book is to inspire.
It is to remind you of your inborn, innate capacity
to heal. Every person writing had a choice.
They chose chiropractic with amazing results."

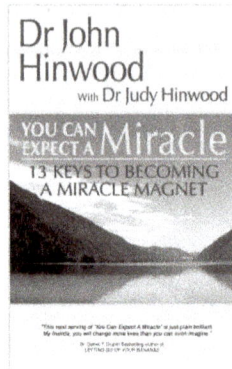

Dr John
Hinwood
with Dr Judy Hinwood

YOU CAN EXPECT A Miracle
13 KEYS TO BECOMING
A MIRACLE MAGNET

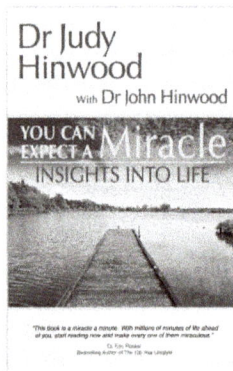

Dr Judy
Hinwood
with Dr John Hinwood

YOU CAN EXPECT A Miracle
INSIGHTS INTO LIFE

Available on www.amazon.com or www.expectamiracle.com

One Last Thing ...

I would like to thank you for taking the time to read this book. I am sincerely grateful and hope that it has lit a fire of inspiration in you to begin to take the steps necessary to live the fullest, most vibrant life you can!

If this book has touched you personally, made you laugh (or maybe cry!), challenged your thinking, sparked inspiration and hope, provided useful information or has made you think of a friend or family member who could do with this kind of information ...

Please, Please, Please...

Take a few minutes to rate this book. When you turn the page, Kindle will give you the opportunity to do this and to share your thoughts on Facebook, LinkedIn and Twitter. If you believe the book is worth sharing, please take a few seconds to let as many people as possible know about it. This is one small step of service you can take to spread the word.

If it turns out to make a difference in peoples lives, they'll be forever grateful to you, as will I.

Once again, my sincerest gratitude and thanks and best of luck on your journey!

Love & miracles

John Hinwood